Type 2 Diabetes Cookbook for Beginners

2000+ Days of Super Easy, Delicious, Low-Sugar & Low-Carb Recipes, Plus a 30-Day Meal Plan to Manage Type 2 Diabetes and Live a Healthy Lifestyle

Indulge in Wellness: Where Flavor Meets Healthful Living

Levi Reeds

Copyright © 2024 By Levi Reeds. All rights reserved.

No part of this book may be reproduced, transmitted, or distributed in any form or by any means without permission in writing from the publisher, except in the case of brief quotations embodied in critical articles or reviews.

Legal & Disclaimer

The content and information contained in this book has been compiled from reliable sources, which are accurate based on the knowledge, belief, expertise and information of the Author. The author cannot be held liable for any omissions and/or errors.

TABLE OF CONTENTS

INTRODUCTION 7
CHAPTER 1: INTRODUCTION TO DIABETES 8
    Diabetes Explained: Insights into How Diabetes Affects Dietary Choices 8
    Managing Diabetes with Nutrition: The Importance of Diet in Regulating Glucose 9
    New Findings in Diabetes and Dietetics: Analyzing Cutting-Edge Research 10
    The Role of Carbohydrates in Blood Sugar Management: A Comprehensive Guide 11
    Selecting Nutritious Fats and Proteins: Strategies for a Balanced Diet 12
    Navigating Food Labels: Essential Tips for Making Informed Dietary Choices 13
CHAPTER 2: 30-DAY MEAL PLAN 16
CHAPTER 3: BREAKFAST 19
Quick and Nutritious Starts 19
    Sautéed Kale and Cherry Tomato Egg Muffins 19
    Herbed Chicken and Vegetable Breakfast Skillet 19
    Turkey Bacon and Spinach Scramble 20
    Ricotta and Spinach Bake 20
    Low-Carb Zucchini And Cheese Waffles .. 21
    Turkey and Spinach Breakfast Meatballs with Spiced Tomato Sauce 21
    Avocado Toast With Poached Egg and Feta Cheese 22
    Spiced Pumpkin and Cottage Cheese Pancakes 22
    Smoked Salmon and Cream Cheese Omelette 23
    Apple Cinnamon Quinoa Breakfast Bowl .. 23
    Mushroom and Thyme Stuffed Bell Peppers 24
    Mushroom and Swiss Chard Frittata 24
    Cauliflower Hash Browns with Fried Eggs 25
    Roasted Red Pepper and Feta Frittata 25
    Savory Miso Oatmeal with Greens 26
    Blueberry and Lemon Zest Ricotta Crepes ... 26
    Chia Seed And Berry Yogurt Parfait 27
    Cottage Cheese And Walnut Bowl With Berries 27
CHAPTER 4: BREAKFAST 28
Leisurely Weekend Brunch Ideas 28
    Asparagus and Goat Cheese Frittata 28
    Low-Carb Lemon Ricotta Pancakes 28
    Grilled Tomato and Mozzarella Caprese Salad 29
    Grilled Portobello Mushrooms with Poached Eggs 29
    Broccoli and Cheddar Cheese Quiche 30
    Keto-Friendly Bagels with Smoked Salmon Spread 30
    Spinach and Feta Egg Muffins 31
    Black Bean and Corn Breakfast Quesadilla .. 31
    Sundried Tomato and Goat Cheese Breakfast Flatbread 32
    Egg White and Spinach Breakfast Burrito . 32
CHAPTER 5: BREAKFAST 33
Low-Carb Smoothie 33
    Matcha Green Tea and Avocado Smoothie .. 33
    Mixed Berry and Flaxseed Smoothie 33
    Cranberry and Orange Zest Detox Smoothie 34
    Celery and Green Apple Hydration Smoothie 34
CHAPTER 6: LUNCH 35
Salads 35
    Turkey Bacon and Spinach Salad with Boiled Eggs 35
    Buffalo Chicken Salad with Blue Cheese Dressing 35
    Beef Fajita Salad with Avocado Lime Dressing 36
    Balsamic Glazed Portobello Mushroom Salad with Arugula 36
    Grilled Eggplant and Bell Pepper Salad with Feta 37
    Grilled Chicken Salad with Avocado Dressing 37

Grilled Chicken and Avocado Caesar Salad. 38
Salmon Nicoise Salad................38
Southwest Steak Salad................39
Kale, Apple, and Roasted Almond Salad with Feta................39
Cobb Salad with Turkey Bacon................40
Caprese Salad with Grilled Chicken................40

CHAPTER 7: LUNCH................41
Hearty Soups and Stews................41
Hearty Vegetable and Bean Soup................41
Tomato and Basil Bisque with Almond Milk... 41
Chicken and Spinach Soup with Fresh Herbs................42
Turkey and White Bean Chili................42
Greek-Style Lemon and Olive Chicken Stew 43
Hearty Turkey and Vegetable Stew................43
Spicy Chicken and Tomato Stew................44
Pork, Cabbage, and Apple Stew................44
Ratatouille: Mixed Vegetable Stew................45
Moroccan-Spiced Chickpea and Eggplant Stew................45
Beef and Green Bean Stew................46
Beef and Mushroom Stew................46

CHAPTER 8: LUNCH................47
Poultry and Meat Dish................47
Roasted Chicken with Mediterranean Vegetables................47
Lemon Herb Grilled Lamb Chops with Asparagus................47
Cauliflower Shepherd's Pie................48
Meatloaf with Ground Chicken and Spinach. 48
Chicken Tikka Masala with Basmati Rice..49
Beef and Eggplant Casserole................49
Vegetable and Lentil Curry with Brown Rice. 50
Zucchini Noodles with Turkey Meatballs in a Low-Sugar Marinara Sauce................50
Beef and Vegetable Kabobs with a Side of Greek Yogurt Tzatziki................51
Herb-Roasted Pork Loin with Apples and Parsnips................51
Steak Fajita Bowls with Cilantro Lime Rice... 52
Stuffed Bell Peppers with Ground Turkey and Quinoa................52

CHAPTER 9: SNACK................53
Healthy Snack Options................53
Almond and Chia Seed Energy Balls........53
Avocado and Lime Mousse................53
Avocado and Cottage Cheese Dip................54
Baked Eggplant Rounds with Low-Carb Marinara Sauce................54
Garlic and Herb Baked Ricotta................55
Stuffed Tomatoes with Herbed Cream Cheese................55
Creamy Spinach and Artichoke Dip................56
Sundried Tomato and Basil Hummus with Whole Grain Crackers................56
Low-Carb Salsa Verde with Baked Chicken Thighs................57
Zesty Lemon and Thyme Tapenade................57

CHAPTER 10: DESSERTS AND BAKED GOODS. 58
Guilt-Free Sweet Treats................58
Orange and Almond Flour Cake................58
No-Bake Peanut Butter Balls................58
Keto-Friendly Cheesecake with Almond Crust................59
Almond Flour Chocolate Chip Cookies.....59
Raspberry Almond Flour Scones................60
Sugar-Free Lemon Bars................60
Coconut and Chia Seed Pudding................61
Sugar-Free Lemon Ricotta Cheesecake...61

CHAPTER 11: DESSERTS AND BAKED GOODS. 62
Baked Goods and Pastries................62
Low-Carb Lemon Ricotta Cake................62
Coconut and Raspberry Friands................62
Sugar-Free Cranberry and Orange Loaf...63
Almond and Orange Zest Biscotti................63

CHAPTER 12: DESSERTS AND BAKED GOODS. 64
Frozen Desserts and Puddings................64
Keto Lemon and Blueberry Frozen Yogurt 64
Mixed Berry Coconut Milk Sherbet................64
Almond Milk and Vanilla Bean Panna Cotta.. 65
Sugar-Free Mint Chocolate Chip Ice Cream.

CHAPTER 13: DINNER 66
Simple Weeknight Dinners 66
- Mediterranean-Style Baked Cod with Tomatoes and Olives 66
- Grilled Salmon with Avocado Salsa 66
- Lemon Herb Cod with Cauliflower Mash ... 67
- Garlic Shrimp Zoodles with Pesto 67
- Seafood Paella with Brown Rice 68
- Spicy Tuna Stuffed Avocados 68

CHAPTER 14: DINNER 69
Vegetable Evening Feasts 69
- Grilled Zucchini and Bell Pepper with Feta ... 69
- Cucumber and Yogurt Salad with Dill 69
- Quinoa Salad with Roasted Vegetables 70
- Eggplant and Zucchini Lasagna 70
- Spinach and Feta Stuffed Portobello Mushrooms 71
- Broccoli and Couscous Salad with Honey Mustard Dressing 71

CHAPTER 15: DINNER 72
Sea Special Occasion Dishes 72
- Chilean Sea Bass with Pomegranate Salsa and Couscous 72
- Oyster Mushroom and Spinach Stuffed Salmon 72
- Salmon en Papillote with Vegetables 73
- Grilled Swordfish with Mediterranean Salsa. 73
- Tilapia with Fennel and Orange Salad 74
- Herb-Crusted Haddock with Steamed Vegetables 74
- Baked Stuffed Flounder with Spinach and Feta 75
- Miso Glazed Halibut with Bok Choy Stir-Fry. 75
- Blackened Swordfish with Mango Avocado Salsa 76
- Broiled Haddock with Spinach and Feta Salad 76
- Honey Mustard Glazed Trout with Green Beans 77
- Paprika Spiced Sole with Roasted Garlic Broccoli 77

CHAPTER 16: DINNER 78
Low-Carb Pastas and Risottos 78
- Spaghetti Squash with Homemade Marinara Sauce 78
- Pasta alla Norma with Eggplant and Ricotta. 78
- Lemon and Asparagus Risotto 79
- Creamy Spinach and Mushroom Risotto (Cauliflower Rice) 79

CHAPTER 17: BONUSES 80
Meal Plans and Shopping Templates: Convenient Tools for Stress-Free Meal Planning 80
- Grocery Shopping List for 7-Day Meal Plan .. 80
- Grocery Shopping List for 8-14 Day Meal Plan 81
- Grocery Shopping List for 15-21 Day Meal Plan 82
- Grocery Shopping List for 22-28 Day Meal Plan 83

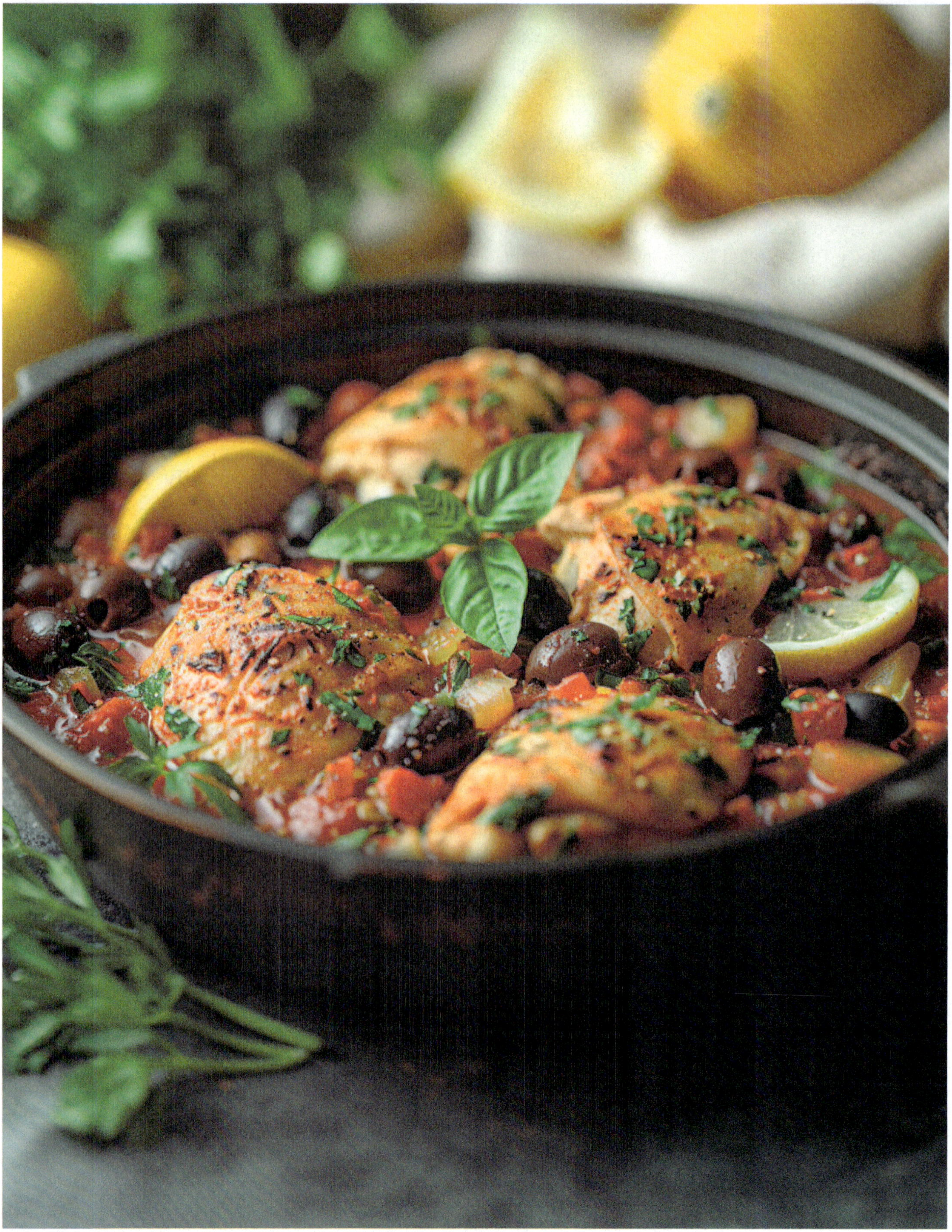

INTRODUCTION

Dear readers,

Welcome to "The Complete Diabetic Cookbook for Beginners" by Levi Reeds. It is an essential guide for anyone newly diagnosed with diabetes or looking to manage their condition through diet. Levi Reeds, a renowned expert in nutrition and health, provides a comprehensive yet easy-to-follow guide for those who are venturing into the world of diabetic-friendly cooking for the first time.

This cookbook is designed to simplify meal planning for individuals with diabetes, offering a wide range of delicious and nutritious recipes that cater to various tastes and dietary needs. Each recipe includes detailed nutritional information, helping readers make informed choices about their meals. Whether you're looking for hearty breakfasts, satisfying main courses, or indulgent yet healthy desserts, this book has it all.

With "Diabetic Cookbook for Beginners," Levi Reeds aims to show that a diabetes diagnosis doesn't mean the end of enjoying food. Instead, it's an opportunity to discover new favorites and learn how to make meals that are both healthful and enjoyable. This book is more than just a collection of recipes; it's a tool for empowering individuals to take control of their health and well-being through the food they eat.

CHAPTER 1: INTRODUCTION TO DIABETES

Diabetes Explained: Insights into How Diabetes Affects Dietary Choices

Understanding Diabetes

Before diving into the specifics of a diabetic diet, it's crucial to understand what diabetes is. Diabetes is a chronic medical condition where the body either doesn't produce enough insulin or can't use it effectively. Insulin is a hormone that regulates blood sugar, or glucose, which is vital for our bodies to produce energy.

There are two main types of diabetes: Type 1, where the body doesn't produce insulin, and Type 2, where the body doesn't use insulin properly. Both types lead to high levels of glucose in the blood, which can cause a range of health issues over time.

The Impact of Diabetes on Nutrition

Living with diabetes doesn't just affect how you feel – it changes how your body processes food. When your insulin levels are unbalanced, it's harder for your body to convert food into energy. This is why dietary choices are a key component of managing diabetes.

For someone with diabetes, it's not just about avoiding sugar. It's about understanding how different types of food affect blood sugar levels. Carbohydrates, for example, break down into glucose in your body and can cause blood sugar levels to rise. Therefore, managing carbohydrate intake is essential in a diabetic diet.

The Role of Diet in Managing Diabetes

A well-planned diabetic diet can help control blood sugar levels, maintain healthy weight, and reduce the risk of diabetes-related complications. The goals are simple: stabilize blood sugar levels, provide necessary nutrients, and align with the individual's lifestyle and preferences.

A diabetic diet isn't a one-size-fits-all solution. It varies depending on the type of diabetes, the individual's age, weight, activity level, and other health conditions. However, there are general guidelines that everyone can follow.

Key Dietary Considerations

Carbohydrates: It's about the type and quantity of carbohydrates. Whole grains, fruits, and vegetables are better choices than processed foods and sugary snacks.

Proteins and Fats: Opt for lean proteins and healthy fats. These can help control blood sugar levels and promote satiety without spiking glucose levels.

Portion Control: Understanding portion sizes is crucial in managing calorie intake and blood sugar levels.

Regular Meals: Eating at regular intervals helps maintain steady blood sugar levels.

The First Steps

Starting a diabetic diet involves learning about different food groups and how they affect your blood sugar. It also means becoming comfortable with reading food labels and understanding nutritional information.

Consulting with a healthcare provider or a dietitian can provide personalized dietary advice. They can help you develop a meal plan that fits your specific needs and lifestyle.

Managing Diabetes with Nutrition: The Importance of Diet in Regulating Glucose

The Power of Diet in Diabetes Control
Effective management of diabetes is not just about taking medication; it's also heavily reliant on dietary choices. What, when, and how much you eat plays a crucial role in regulating your blood glucose levels. This chapter focuses on understanding how a balanced diet can become a powerful tool in managing diabetes.

Building a Balanced Diet

A diabetic diet is more about balance and consistency rather than deprivation. Here are the key components:

Carbohydrates: Carbs have the most significant impact on blood sugar levels. Choose complex carbohydrates like whole grains, fruits, and vegetables, which take longer to digest and cause a slower, more manageable rise in blood sugar.

Fiber: High-fiber foods not only aid in digestion but also help to regulate blood sugar levels. Foods like beans, legumes, whole grains, nuts, seeds, fruits, and vegetables are excellent fiber sources.

Proteins: Lean proteins (like chicken, fish, and plant-based proteins) are an essential part of a diabetic diet. They have minimal impact on blood sugar levels and can help in maintaining muscle mass and overall health.

Fats: Focus on healthy fats from sources like avocados, nuts, seeds, and olive oil. These fats don't raise blood sugar and can help with satiety and flavor.

Timing and Portion Control

Consistent meal timing and appropriate portion sizes can help in stabilizing blood sugar levels throughout the day. Skipping meals or overeating can lead to significant fluctuations in glucose levels, which can be harmful.

Understanding the Glycemic Index

The Glycemic Index (GI) is a valuable tool for people with diabetes. It rates how quickly foods raise blood sugar levels. Low-GI foods are absorbed more slowly, helping to maintain more stable blood sugar levels.

Hydration

Staying hydrated is vital. Water is the best beverage choice for most people with diabetes. Avoid sugary drinks like sodas, fruit juices, and sweetened teas as they can cause a rapid increase in blood sugar levels.

The Role of Meal Planning

Planning your meals can make a significant difference. It helps in maintaining a balanced diet and ensures that you have the right kinds of food on hand. Meal planning can also aid in managing portion sizes and avoiding impulsive eating.

Making Dietary Adjustments

Adjusting to a diabetic diet can be a process. Start small – make gradual changes rather than overhauling your diet overnight. It's also important to monitor your blood sugar levels to see how different foods affect you.

Involving a Healthcare Professional

Consulting with a registered dietitian or a diabetes educator can provide customized dietary advice. They can help you understand your specific nutritional needs and create a diet plan that suits your lifestyle and preferences.

New Findings in Diabetes and Dietetics: Analyzing Cutting-Edge Research

Embracing Emerging Science in Diabetes Management

As our understanding of diabetes evolves, so do the strategies for managing it. This chapter delves into the latest research findings in the field of diabetes and dietetics, highlighting how these insights can shape the approach to a diabetic diet.

Personalized Nutrition: The Frontier of Diabetes Care

One of the most significant advancements in diabetes management is the move towards personalized nutrition. Cutting-edge research suggests that individuals respond differently to various foods based on genetic, metabolic, and environmental factors. This personalized approach can lead to more effective diet plans tailored to individual needs and responses.

The Role of Gut Microbiota

Recent studies have shed light on the crucial role of gut microbiota in glucose metabolism and diabetes management. A diverse and balanced gut microbiome has been linked to improved blood sugar control and reduced inflammation. Foods rich in probiotics (like yogurt and kefir) and prebiotics (such as garlic, onions, and bananas) can help in cultivating a healthy gut environment.

Advanced Carbohydrate Understanding

Innovations in carbohydrate research go beyond the traditional categorization of simple and complex carbs. Scientists are now exploring how different types of carbohydrates and their food sources impact blood glucose levels and diabetes risk. This research underscores the importance of the quality and source of carbohydrates in a diabetic diet.

Impact of Plant-based Diets

Emerging research highlights the benefits of plant-based diets in managing diabetes. These diets are rich in fiber, vitamins, and minerals, and low in saturated fats. Studies show that a plant-based diet can improve blood sugar control, aid in weight management, and reduce the risk of heart disease.

The Potential of Functional Foods

Functional foods, those containing bioactive compounds with health benefits, are gaining attention in diabetes management. Foods like berries, nuts, seeds, and green leafy vegetables are being studied for their potential to improve insulin sensitivity and reduce oxidative stress and inflammation.

Intermittent Fasting and Diabetes

Intermittent fasting, a dietary pattern that cycles between periods of fasting and eating, has been explored for its potential benefits in improving insulin sensitivity and reducing blood sugar levels. However, it's essential to approach intermittent fasting cautiously and under medical supervision, especially for individuals with diabetes.

Technology in Dietary Management

Technology plays an increasingly vital role in managing diabetes. Apps and devices that track food intake, monitor blood glucose levels, and provide nutritional advice are becoming indispensable tools in personalized diabetes care.

The Importance of Continuous Learning

The field of diabetes and nutrition is rapidly evolving. It's crucial for individuals with diabetes and healthcare professionals to stay informed about the latest research and how it can be applied to dietary management.

The Role of Carbohydrates in Blood Sugar Management: A Comprehensive Guide

Understanding Carbohydrates in Diabetes

Carbohydrates play a pivotal role in blood sugar management, making them a key focus for anyone beginning a diabetic diet. This chapter provides a comprehensive guide to understanding carbohydrates and their impact on diabetes.

The Basics of Carbohydrates

Carbohydrates are one of the primary macronutrients found in food, alongside proteins and fats. They are your body's main source of energy and are broken down into glucose, which enters the bloodstream and raises blood sugar levels. There are two main types of carbohydrates: simple and complex.

Simple Carbohydrates: These are quickly broken down and can cause rapid spikes in blood sugar. They are found in sugary foods and drinks, as well as some fruits and dairy products.

Complex Carbohydrates: These are broken down more slowly, leading to a gradual rise in blood sugar. They are found in foods like whole grains, legumes, and vegetables.

Glycemic Index and Glycemic Load

The glycemic index (GI) is a measure of how quickly a carbohydrate-containing food raises blood sugar levels. Foods with a high GI spike blood sugar rapidly, while low GI foods have a slower, more gradual impact. Glycemic load (GL) takes into account the amount of carbohydrate in a portion of food, giving a more accurate picture of its impact on blood sugar.

Balancing Carbohydrates in Your Diet

It's important for beginners to understand how to balance carbohydrate intake:

Choose Low-GI Foods: Opt for whole grains, legumes, fruits, and vegetables.

Portion Control: Be mindful of the portion sizes of carbohydrate-rich foods to avoid blood sugar spikes.

Distribute Carbohydrates Evenly: Spread carbohydrate intake evenly throughout the day to maintain steady blood sugar levels.

The Importance of Fiber

High-fiber foods, which are often rich in complex carbohydrates, can slow the absorption of sugar in the bloodstream and can be beneficial for blood sugar control. Incorporating fiber-rich foods into your diet is essential for effective diabetes management.

Carbohydrates and Meal Planning

When planning meals, consider the type and amount of carbohydrates. A balanced plate should include a mix of carbohydrates, protein, and healthy fats. This balance helps in regulating blood sugar and providing essential nutrients.

Monitoring and Adjusting

Learning to manage carbohydrate intake is a process. Regular blood sugar monitoring can help in understanding how your body responds to different types and amounts of carbohydrates, allowing you to make necessary adjustments.

Involving a Healthcare Professional

Working with a healthcare provider or a dietitian can help in creating a personalized carbohydrate management plan, considering individual needs, preferences, and lifestyle.

Selecting Nutritious Fats and Proteins: Strategies for a Balanced Diet

The Importance of Fats and Proteins in a Diabetic Diet

While much attention is given to carbohydrates in diabetes management, fats and proteins are equally important. They play crucial roles in overall health and can affect blood sugar levels indirectly. This chapter provides strategies for incorporating healthy fats and proteins into a diabetic diet.

Understanding Healthy Fats

Fats have often been misunderstood. In reality, healthy fats are essential for nutrient absorption, brain health, and heart health. For people with diabetes, choosing the right type of fat is key.

Monounsaturated Fats: Found in olive oil, avocados, and nuts, these fats can improve heart health and stabilize blood sugar levels.

Polyunsaturated Fats: Including omega-3 and omega-6 fatty acids, these are found in fatty fish, flaxseeds, and walnuts and are beneficial for heart health.

Saturated and Trans Fats: Often found in processed foods, these should be limited as they can increase the risk of heart disease.

The Role of Protein

Protein is important for repairing tissues and maintaining muscle mass. It has a minimal impact on blood sugar levels, making it a key component of a diabetic diet.

Animal Proteins: Choose lean options like chicken, turkey, and fish. Red meat should be eaten in moderation.

Plant-based Proteins: Beans, lentils, tofu, and quinoa are excellent protein sources and also provide fiber and other nutrients.

Balancing Fats and Proteins with Carbohydrates

In a diabetic diet, it's not just about choosing healthy fats and proteins but also balancing them with carbohydrates. This balance helps in managing blood sugar levels and providing sustained energy.

Cooking and Preparation Methods

The way food is prepared can impact its nutritional value. Grilling, baking, steaming, and sautéing are healthier cooking methods compared to frying. Use herbs and spices for flavoring instead of relying on salt or sugar-heavy sauces.

Portion Sizes and Meal Planning

Paying attention to portion sizes is essential, especially for high-calorie foods like nuts and cheeses. Incorporating a variety of fats and proteins throughout the day ensures nutritional balance.

The Impact of Fats and Proteins on Blood Sugar

Although fats and proteins don't raise blood sugar levels as carbohydrates do, they can affect how the body uses insulin. Therefore, it's important to monitor blood sugar responses and make dietary adjustments as needed.

Involving a Healthcare Professional

Consulting with a dietitian can help in understanding how to integrate healthy fats and proteins into your diet in a way that supports blood sugar management and overall health.

Navigating Food Labels: Essential Tips for Making Informed Dietary Choices

The Significance of Reading Food Labels in Diabetes Management

For individuals beginning a diabetic diet, understanding food labels is a crucial skill. Food labels provide vital information about the nutritional content of foods, helping you make informed choices that align with your dietary needs. This chapter offers key insights into interpreting these labels effectively.

Breaking Down the Nutrition Facts Label

Most packaged foods come with a Nutrition Facts label. Here's how to read and understand the key components:

Serving Size: This indicates the amount typically consumed in one sitting. All the nutritional information on the label is based on this serving size.

Total Carbohydrates: Pay attention to this number as it directly affects blood sugar levels. It includes all types of carbohydrates – sugars, complex carbohydrates, and fiber.

Fiber: High fiber content is beneficial for blood sugar control. Fiber is subtracted from the total carbohydrates to calculate "net carbs".

Sugars: This includes both added sugars and natural sugars. Opt for foods with low added sugars.

Protein: Consider the protein content, especially in relation to the total carbohydrates, as protein can help balance blood sugar levels.

Fats: Look at the type and amount of fat. Prefer foods with healthier fats (monounsaturated and polyunsaturated).

Ingredients List

The ingredients list is as important as the nutrition facts. Ingredients are listed in order of quantity, from highest to lowest. Look for whole food ingredients and be cautious of added sugars and unhealthy fats.

Understanding Health Claims

Be wary of health claims on labels. Terms like "low-fat" or "sugar-free" can be misleading. "Low-fat" products might be high in sugar, and "sugar-free" products can still impact blood sugar due to other carbohydrates.

Special Labels: 'Diabetic-friendly' and 'No Added Sugar'

Products labeled as "diabetic-friendly" or "no added sugar" can still affect blood sugar levels. Always read the nutritional facts and ingredients to understand the overall carbohydrate content.

The Role of Allergen Information

For those with food allergies, the allergen information is crucial. This section of the label indicates the presence of common allergens like nuts, dairy, or gluten.

Technology Aids in Label Reading

Apps and tools are available to help interpret food labels and track your intake. These can be especially helpful for beginners in a diabetic diet.

Practicing Label Reading

Familiarize yourself with reading food labels during your shopping trips. Over time, this practice becomes second nature, aiding significantly in making diabetes-friendly dietary choices.

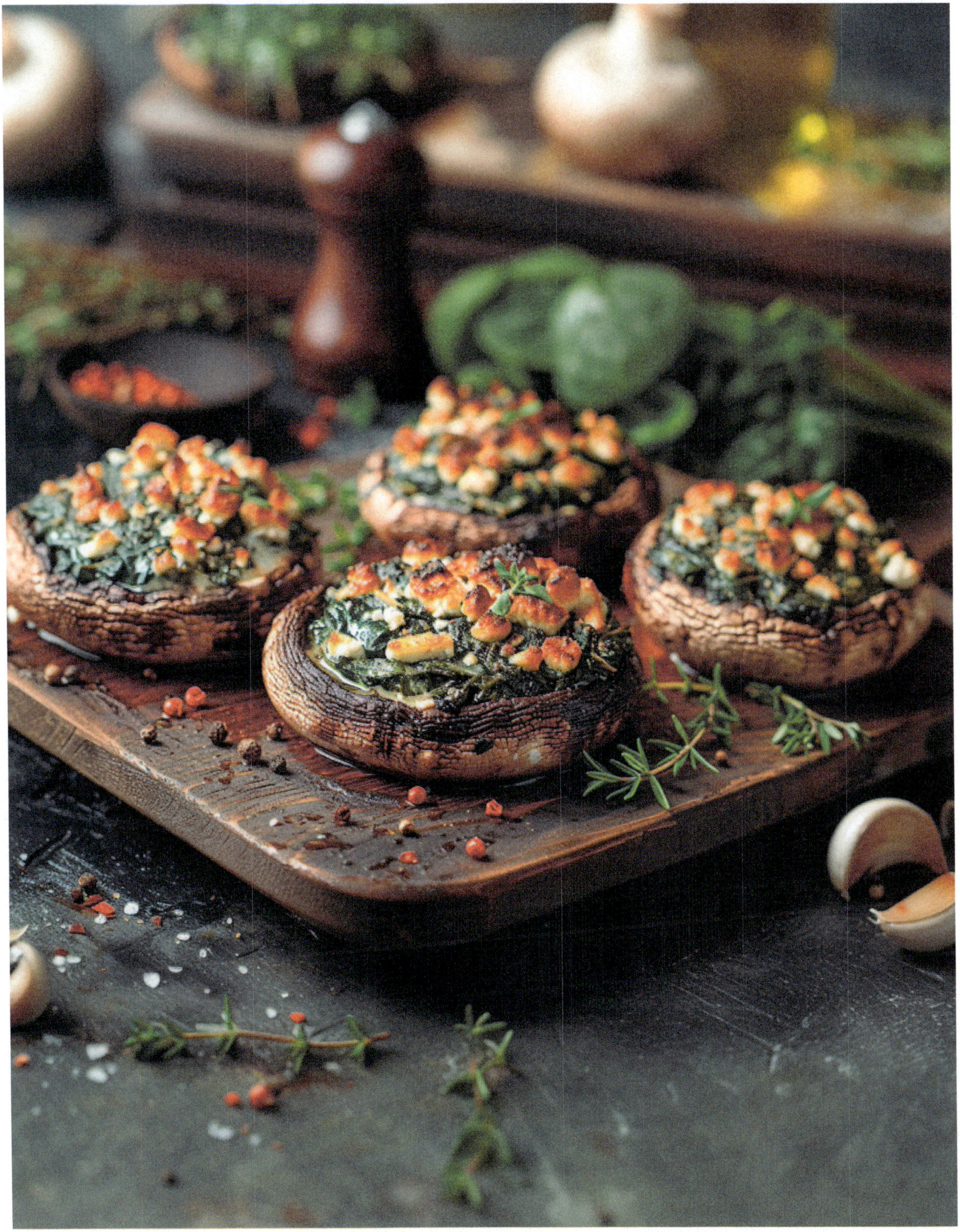

CHAPTER 2: 30-DAY MEAL PLAN

Day	Breakfast (400 kcal)	Lunch (500 kcal)	Snack (220 kcal)	Dinner (380 kcal)
Day 1	Sautéed Kale and Cherry Tomato Egg Muffins - p.19	Turkey Bacon and Spinach Salad with Boiled Eggs - p.35	Almond and Chia Seed Energy Balls - p.53	Mediterranean-Style Baked Cod with Tomatoes and Olives - p.66
Day 2	Blueberry and Lemon Zest Ricotta Crepes - p.26	Beef Fajita Salad with Avocado Lime Dressing - p.36	Avocado and Cottage Cheese Dip - p.54	Grilled Zucchini and Bell Pepper with Feta - p.69
Day 3	Turkey Bacon and Spinach Scramble - p.20	Chicken and Spinach Soup with Fresh Herbs - p.42	Garlic and Herb Baked Ricotta - p.55	Herb-Crusted Haddock with Steamed Vegetables - p.74
Day 4	Matcha Green Tea and Avocado Smoothie - p.33	Grilled Chicken Salad with Avocado Dressing - p.37	Coconut and Chia Seed Pudding - p.61	Baked Stuffed Flounder with Spinach and Feta - p.75
Day 5	Low-Carb Lemon Ricotta Pancakes - p.28	Greek-Style Lemon and Olive Chicken Stew - p.43	Creamy Spinach and Artichoke Dip - p.56	Cauliflower Shepherd's Pie - p.48
Day 6	Herbed Chicken and Vegetable Breakfast Skillet - p.19	Ratatouille: Mixed Vegetable Stew - p.45	Sundried Tomato and Basil Hummus with Whole Grain Crackers - p.56	Salmon en Papillote with Vegetables - p.73
Day 7	Avocado Toast with Poached Egg and Feta Cheese - p.22	Buffalo Chicken Salad with Blue Cheese Dressing - p.35	Keto-Friendly Cheesecake with Almond Crust - p.59	Lemon Herb Grilled Lamb Chops with Asparagus - p.47
Day 8	Chia Seed And Berry Yogurt Parfait - p.27	Turkey and White Bean Chili - p.42	Zesty Lemon and Thyme Tapenade - p.57	Spaghetti Squash with Homemade Marinara Sauce - p.78
Day 9	Ricotta and Spinach Bake - p.20	Balsamic Glazed Portobello Mushroom Salad with Arugula - p.36	Avocado and Lime Mousse - p.53	Blackened Swordfish with Mango Avocado Salsa - p.76
Day 10	Spiced Pumpkin and Cottage Cheese Pancakes - p.22	Beef and Green Bean Stew - p.46	No-Bake Peanut Butter Balls - p.58	Broccoli and Couscous Salad with Honey Mustard Dressing - p.71
Day 11	Smoked Salmon and Cream Cheese Omelette - p.23	Grilled Eggplant and Bell Pepper Salad with Feta - p.37	Stuffed Tomatoes with Herbed Cream Cheese - p.55	Grilled Swordfish with Mediterranean Salsa - p.73
Day 12	Mushroom and Thyme Stuffed Bell Peppers - p.24	Southwest Steak Salad - p.39	Raspberry Almond Flour Scones - p.60	Paprika Spiced Sole with Roasted Garlic Broccoli - p.77
Day 13	Apple Cinnamon Quinoa Breakfast Bowl - p.23	Moroccan-Spiced Chickpea and Eggplant Stew - p.45	Mixed Berry Coconut Milk Sherbet - p.64	Meatloaf with Ground Chicken and Spinach - p.48
Day 14	Mushroom and Swiss Chard Frittata - p.24	Grilled Chicken and Avocado Caesar Salad - p.38	Low-Carb Salsa Verde with Baked Chicken Thighs - p.57	Chilean Sea Bass with Pomegranate Salsa and Couscous - p.72
Day 15	Celery and Green Apple Hydration Smoothie - p.34	Pork, Cabbage, and Apple Stew - p.44	Sugar-Free Lemon Bars - p.60	Broiled Haddock with Spinach and Feta Salad - p.76

Day	Breakfast (400 kcal)	Lunch (500 kcal)	Snack (220 kcal)	Dinner (380 kcal)
Day 16	Roasted Red Pepper and Feta Frittata - p.25	Caprese Salad with Grilled Chicken - p.40	Almond Flour Chocolate Chip Cookies - p.59	Herb-Roasted Pork Loin with Apples and Parsnips - p.51
Day 17	Savory Miso Oatmeal with Greens - p.26	Tomato and Basil Bisque with Almond Milk - p.41	Coconut and Raspberry Friands - p.62	Zucchini Noodles with Turkey Meatballs in a Low-Sugar Marinara Sauce - p.50
Day 18	Cauliflower Hash Browns with Fried Eggs - p.25	Kale, Apple, and Roasted Almond Salad with Feta - p.39	Creamy Spinach and Artichoke Dip - p.56	Miso Glazed Halibut with Bok Choy Stir-Fry - p.75
Day 19	Spinach and Feta Egg Muffins - p.31	Salmon Nicoise Salad - p.38	Avocado and Cottage Cheese Dip - p.54	Vegetable and Lentil Curry with Brown Rice - p.50
Day 20	Black Bean and Corn Breakfast Quesadilla - p.31	Cobb Salad with Turkey Bacon - p.40	Sugar-Free Cranberry and Orange Loaf - p.63	Tilapia with Fennel and Orange Salad - p.74
Day 21	Grilled Portobello Mushrooms with Poached Eggs - p.29	Beef and Mushroom Stew - p.46	Garlic and Herb Baked Ricotta - p.55	Chicken Tikka Masala with Basmati Rice - p.49
Day 22	Egg White and Spinach Breakfast Burrito - p.32	Hearty Vegetable and Bean Soup - p.41	Keto Lemon and Blueberry Frozen Yogurt - p.64	Steak Fajita Bowls with Cilantro Lime Rice - p.52
Day 23	Mixed Berry and Flaxseed Smoothie - p.33	Hearty Turkey and Vegetable Stew - p.43	Creamy Spinach and Artichoke Dip - p.56	Baked Stuffed Flounder with Spinach and Feta - p.75
Day 24	Grilled Tomato and Mozzarella Caprese Salad - p.29	Grilled Chicken Salad with Avocado Dressing - p.37	Coconut and Chia Seed Pudding - p.61	Grilled Salmon with Avocado Salsa - p.66
Day 25	Low-Carb Smoothie - p.33	Spicy Chicken and Tomato Stew - p.44	Orange and Almond Flour Cake - p.58	Herb-Crusted Haddock with Steamed Vegetables - p.74
Day 26	Broccoli and Cheddar Cheese Quiche - p.30	Grilled Eggplant and Bell Pepper Salad with Feta - p.37	Stuffed Tomatoes with Herbed Cream Cheese - p.55	Baked Stuffed Flounder with Spinach and Feta - p.75
Day 27	Sundried Tomato and Goat Cheese Breakfast Flatbread - p.32	Grilled Chicken Salad with Avocado Dressing - p.37	Zesty Lemon and Thyme Tapenade - p.57	Zucchini Noodles with Turkey Meatballs in a Low-Sugar Marinara Sauce - p.50
Day 28	Low-Carb Zucchini And Cheese Waffles - p.21	Ratatouille: Mixed Vegetable Stew - p.45	Coconut and Raspberry Friands - p.62	Chilean Sea Bass with Pomegranate Salsa and Couscous - p.72
Day 29	Sundried Tomato and Goat Cheese Breakfast Flatbread - p.32	Turkey and White Bean Chili - p.42	Garlic and Herb Baked Ricotta - p.55	Mediterranean-Style Baked Cod with Tomatoes and Olives - p.66
Day 30	Spinach and Feta Egg Muffins - p.31	Beef Fajita Salad with Avocado Lime Dressing - p.36	Creamy Spinach and Artichoke Dip - p.56	Lemon Herb Cod with Cauliflower Mash - p.67

Important Reminder: The 30-Day Meal Plan featured in this book is meant to serve as a flexible guide and source of meal inspiration. Please note that the caloric values provided are estimates and can vary based on portion sizes and the specific ingredients you use. Our aim with this meal plan is to offer a well-rounded menu that includes a variety of proteins, healthy fats, and carbohydrates, ensuring you can maintain a balanced diet while still savoring flavorful meals every day.

If you find that the calorie counts in the recipes differ from what you require, feel free to adjust portion sizes accordingly. You are welcome to increase or reduce quantities to better match your individual dietary needs and goals. Don't hesitate to get creative and customize each dish to suit your preferences and enjoy every meal to the fullest!

CHAPTER 3: BREAKFAST
Quick and Nutritious Starts

Sautéed Kale and Cherry Tomato Egg Muffins

Prep: 15 minutes | Cook: 20 minutes | Serves: 6

Ingredients:

- 6 eggs (330g)
- 1 cup kale, chopped (67g)
- 1/2 cup cherry tomatoes, halved (100g)
- 1/4 cup feta cheese, crumbled (50g)
- 1 tbsp olive oil (15ml)
- Salt and pepper to taste

Instructions:

1. Preheat the oven to 350°F (175°C). Grease a muffin tin.
2. Sauté kale in olive oil until wilted. Add cherry tomatoes and cook for 2 more minutes.
3. Divide the kale and tomatoes evenly among the muffin cups.
4. Beat the eggs and pour over the kale and tomatoes. Top with feta cheese.
5. Bake for 15-20 minutes or until set.

Nutrition Facts (Per Serving): Calories: 150 | Fat: 10g | Carbohydrates: 4g | Protein: 12g | Fiber: 1g | Sugars: 2g | Sodium: 200mg

Herbed Chicken and Vegetable Breakfast Skillet

Prep: 15 minutes | Cook: 20 minutes | Serves: 4

Ingredients:

- 1 lb chicken breast, diced (450g)
- 1 cup bell peppers, diced (150g)
- 1 cup zucchini, diced (120g)
- 1/4 cup onion, diced (40g)
- 2 tbsp fresh herbs (parsley, thyme), chopped (6g)
- 2 tbsp olive oil (30ml)
- Salt and pepper to taste

Instructions:

1. Heat olive oil in a skillet over medium heat. Sauté onion until translucent.
2. Add chicken and cook until no longer pink.
3. Add bell peppers and zucchini, cooking until vegetables are tender.
4. Stir in fresh herbs, salt, and pepper.

Nutrition Facts (Per Serving): Calories: 250 | Fat: 10g | Carbohydrates: 6g | Protein: 35g | Fiber: 2g | Sugars: 3g | Sodium: 200mg

Turkey Bacon and Spinach Scramble

Prep: 10 minutes | Cook: 10 minutes | Serves: 1

Ingredients:

- 3 slices turkey bacon (90g)
- 1.5 cups fresh spinach (45g)
- 3 eggs (150g)
- 1 tbsp olive oil (15ml)
- Salt and pepper to taste

Instructions:

1. Cook turkey bacon in a skillet until crispy; set aside.
2. In the same skillet, sauté spinach in olive oil.
3. Beat eggs and pour over spinach; scramble together.
4. Crumble the cooked bacon into the scramble.
5. Season with salt and pepper, and serve.

Nutrition Facts (Per Serving): Calories: 400 | Fat: 30g | Carbohydrates: 3g | Protein: 32g | Fiber: 2g | Sugars: 1g | Sodium: 450mg

Ricotta and Spinach Bake

Prep: 15 minutes | Cook: 30 minutes | Serves: 1

Ingredients:

- 1 cup ricotta cheese (250g)
- 1 cup fresh spinach, chopped (30g)
- 1 egg (50g)
- 1/4 cup grated Parmesan cheese (25g)
- 1/2 tsp nutmeg (1.3g)
- Salt and pepper to taste

Instructions:

1. Preheat oven to 350°F (175°C).
2. Mix spinach, ricotta, Parmesan, eggs, salt, pepper, and nutmeg in a bowl.
3. Pour into a greased baking dish.
4. Bake for 30 minutes until set and lightly golden.
5. Serve warm.

Nutrition Facts (Per Serving): Calories: 400 | Fat: 28g | Carbohydrates: 12g | Protein: 28g | Fiber: 1g | Sugars: 3g | Sodium: 500mg

Low-Carb Zucchini And Cheese Waffles

Prep: 15 minutes | Cook: 10 minutes | Serves: 1

Ingredients:

- 1 cup grated zucchini (squeezed to remove moisture) (120g)
- 1 cup almond flour (100g)
- 1 cup shredded cheddar cheese (low-fat) (100g)
- 4 large eggs
- Salt and pepper to taste
- Non-stick cooking spray

Instructions:

1. In a bowl, mix the grated zucchini, almond flour, cheddar cheese, and eggs. Season with salt and pepper.
2. Preheat the waffle maker and spray with non-stick cooking spray.
3. Scoop the mixture into the waffle maker and close the lid.
4. Cook for about 5 minutes or until the waffles are golden and cooked through.
5. Serve immediately.

Nutrition Facts (Per Serving): Calories: 400 | Fat: 30g | Carbohydrates: 12g | Protein: 28g | Fiber: 6g | Sugars: 3g | Sodium: 400mg

Turkey and Spinach Breakfast Meatballs with Spiced Tomato Sauce

Prep: 15 minutes | Cook: 20 minutes | Serves: 4

Ingredients:

- 1 lb ground turkey (450g)
- 2 cups spinach, finely chopped (60g)
- 1 egg
- 1/4 cup whole-wheat breadcrumbs (30g)
- 1 tsp garlic powder (3g)
- 1 cup tomato sauce (low-sugar) (240ml)
- 1 tsp cumin (2g)
- 1 tsp smoked paprika (2g)
- Salt and pepper to taste

Instructions:

1. Preheat the oven to 375°F (190°C).
2. Mix ground turkey, spinach, egg, breadcrumbs, garlic powder, salt, and pepper. Form into meatballs.
3. Place meatballs on a baking sheet and bake for 15-20 minutes.
4. Heat tomato sauce with cumin and smoked paprika.
5. Serve meatballs topped with spiced tomato sauce.

Nutrition Facts (Per Serving): Calories: 400 | Fat: 20g | Carbohydrates: 18g | Protein: 35g | Fiber: 3g | Sugars: 4g | Sodium: 420mg

Avocado Toast With Poached Egg and Feta Cheese

Prep: 10 minutes | Cook: 5 minutes | Serves: 1

Ingredients:

- 1 slice whole-grain bread
- 1/2 ripe avocado (100g)
- 1 large egg
- 1/4 cup crumbled feta cheese (30g)
- Salt and pepper to taste
- Optional: Chili flakes or herbs for garnish

Instructions:

1. Toast the bread slice until golden and crispy.
2. Mash the avocado and spread it evenly on the toast.
3. Poach the egg in simmering water for about 3-4 minutes.
4. Place the poached egg on top of the avocado toast.
5. Sprinkle cup crumbled feta cheese on top.
6. Season with salt, pepper, and optional garnish.

Nutrition Facts (Per Serving): Calories: 400 | Fat: 29g | Carbohydrates: 21g | Protein: 19g | Fiber: 7g | Sugars: 4g | Sodium: 400mg

Spiced Pumpkin and Cottage Cheese Pancakes

Prep: 10 minutes | Cook: 15 minutes | Serves: 4

Ingredients:

- 1 cup pumpkin puree (245g)
- 1/2 cup cottage cheese (115g)
- 2 large eggs
- 1 cup almond flour (96g)
- 2 tsp baking powder (10g)
- 1 tsp cinnamon (2.6g)
- 1/4 tsp nutmeg (0.5g)
- 1 tbsp coconut oil (15ml) for cooking
- Salt to taste

Instructions:

1. Mix pumpkin puree, cottage cheese, and eggs in a bowl.
2. Combine almond flour, baking powder, cinnamon, nutmeg, and a pinch of salt in another bowl.
3. Merge the wet and dry ingredients until a batter forms.
4. Heat coconut oil in a skillet over medium heat. Pour 1/4 cup (60ml) of batter for each pancake. Cook until bubbles form, then flip and cook until golden brown.

Nutrition Facts (Per Serving): Calories: 400 | Fat: 25g | Carbohydrates: 20g | Protein: 20g | Fiber: 6g | Sugars: 4g | Sodium: 300mg

Smoked Salmon and Cream Cheese Omelette

Prep: 10 minutes | Cook: 5 minutes | Serves: 1

Ingredients:

- 3 eggs (150g)
- 2 oz smoked salmon (56g)
- 2 tbsp cream cheese (28g)
- 1 tbsp chopped chives (1g)
- Salt and pepper to taste

Instructions:

1. Whisk eggs with salt and pepper.
2. Cook eggs in a skillet over medium heat until they start to set.
3. Add cream cheese and smoked salmon on top of the omelette.
4. Fold the omelette in half, cook for another minute.
5. Garnish with chives and serve.

Nutrition Facts (Per Serving): Calories: 400 | Fat: 29g | Carbohydrates: 3g | Protein: 31g | Fiber: 0g | Sugars: 2g | Sodium: 720mg

Apple Cinnamon Quinoa Breakfast Bowl

Prep: 5 minutes | Cook: 15 minutes | Serves: 1

Ingredients:

- 1/4 cup quinoa (42.5g)
- 1/2 cup unsweetened almond milk (120ml)
- 1/4 large apple, diced (45g)
- 1/2 tsp cinnamon (1.3g)
- 1 tbsp walnuts, chopped (7.5g)
- 1 tbsp raisins (10g)
- 3/4 tsp honey (3.75ml)

Instructions:

1. Rinse quinoa under cold water.
2. In a saucepan, combine quinoa, almond milk, apple, and cinnamon. Bring to a boil.
3. Reduce heat, cover, and simmer for 15 minutes or until quinoa is cooked and the liquid is absorbed.
4. Stir in walnuts and raisins. Drizzle with honey.
5. Serve warm.

Nutrition Facts (Per Serving): Calories: 235 | Fat: 3g | Carbohydrates: 48g | Protein: 6g | Fiber: 6g | Sugars: 10g | Sodium: 80mg

Mushroom and Thyme Stuffed Bell Peppers

Prep: 20 minutes | Cook: 30 minutes | Serves: 4

Ingredients:

- 4 large bell peppers, halved and seeded
- 1 lb mushrooms, finely chopped (450g)
- 2 tbsp thyme, fresh, chopped (6g)
- 1 cup quinoa, cooked (185g)
- 1 onion, diced (110g)
- 2 cloves garlic, minced (6g)
- 2 tbsp olive oil (30ml)
- 1/2 cup vegetable broth (120ml)
- 1/4 cup grated Parmesan cheese (30g)
- Salt and pepper to taste

Instructions:

1. Preheat the oven to 375°F (190°C).
2. Sauté onion and garlic in olive oil until translucent. Add mushrooms and thyme, cook until mushrooms are soft.
3. Mix in cooked quinoa and vegetable broth, simmer for 5 minutes.
4. Stuff the bell pepper halves with the mushroom-quinoa mixture. Place in a baking dish.
5. Sprinkle with Parmesan cheese. Bake for 25-30 minutes or until peppers are tender.

Nutrition Facts (Per Serving): Calories: 400 | Fat: 15g | Carbohydrates: 35g | Protein: 20g | Fiber: 8g | Sugars: 8g | Sodium: 250mg

Mushroom and Swiss Chard Frittata

Prep: 10 minutes | Cook: 20 minutes | Serves: 2

Ingredients:

- 6 eggs (300g)
- 1 1/2 cups sliced mushrooms (105g)
- 1 1/2 cups chopped Swiss chard (52.5g)
- 1/2 cup shredded cheese (60g)
- 2 tbsp olive oil (30ml)
- Salt and pepper to taste
- 1/4 cup diced bell peppers (37.5g)
- 1/4 cup diced onions (40g)

Instructions:

1. Preheat the oven to 350°F (175°C).
2. In a skillet, heat olive oil and sauté mushrooms and Swiss chard until softened.
3. In a bowl, whisk eggs with salt and pepper.
4. Pour eggs over the vegetables in the skillet.
5. Sprinkle cheese on top and cook for a few minutes until the edges set.
6. Transfer skillet to oven and bake until frittata is set, about 10-15 minutes.
7. Serve warm.

Nutrition Facts (Per Serving): Calories: 400 | Fat: 30g | Carbohydrates: 12g | Protein: 24g | Fiber: 3g | Sugars: 5g | Sodium: 400mg

Cauliflower Hash Browns with Fried Eggs

Prep: 15 minutes | Cook: 10 minutes | Serves: 1

Ingredients:

- 1 cup grated cauliflower (100g)
- 3 large eggs (150g)
- 1 tbsp olive oil (15ml)
- 1/4 cup shredded cheddar cheese (28g)
- Salt and pepper to taste

Instructions:

1. Form grated cauliflower into patties.
2. Heat olive oil in a pan and cook the cauliflower patties until golden brown on each side.
3. Sprinkle cheddar cheese over the patties and let it melt.
4. In the same pan, fry the eggs to your preference.
5. Serve the eggs on top of the cauliflower hash browns.

Nutritional Facts (Per Serving): Calories: 400 | Fat: 27g | Carbohydrates: 12g | Protein: 29g | Fiber: 3g | Sugars: 4g | Sodium: 400mg

Roasted Red Pepper and Feta Frittata

Prep: 10 minutes | Cook: 25 minutes | Serves: 4

Ingredients:

- 8 eggs (440g)
- 1 cup roasted red peppers, chopped (250g)
- 1 cup feta cheese, crumbled (150g)
- 2 tbsp fresh basil, chopped (5g)
- 1 tbsp olive oil (15ml)
- Salt and pepper to taste

Instructions:

1. Preheat the oven to 375°F (190°C).
2. In a bowl, whisk together eggs, salt, and pepper.
3. Heat olive oil in an oven-safe skillet. Add roasted peppers and sauté for a few minutes.
4. Pour the eggs over the peppers. Sprinkle with feta cheese and basil.
5. Cook for 2-3 minutes on the stove, then transfer to the oven. Bake for 20 minutes.

Nutrition Facts (Per Serving): Calories: 400 | Fat: 20g | Carbohydrates: 6g | Protein: 24g | Fiber: 1g | Sugars: 4g | Sodium: 500mg

Savory Miso Oatmeal with Greens

Prep: 5 minutes | Cook: 10 minutes | Serves: 1

Ingredients:

- 1/3 cup rolled oats (33g)
- 1 cup water or low-sodium vegetable broth (240ml)
- 1 tbsp miso paste (18g)
- 1 cup chopped kale or spinach (67g)
- 1/4 cup chopped scallions (25g)
- 1 egg (50g)
- 1 tbsp sesame seeds (9g)
- Salt and pepper to taste

Instructions:

1. Cook oats in water or broth as per package instructions.
2. In a separate pan, lightly beat the egg and scramble until fully cooked.
3. Stir in miso paste, cooked egg, kale or spinach, and scallions into the oatmeal.
4. Cook until the greens are wilted.
5. Garnish with sesame seeds, season with salt and pepper to taste.

Nutritional Facts (Per Serving): Calories: 400 | Fat: 18g | Carbohydrates: 30g | Protein: 23g | Fiber: 6g | Sugars: 4g | Sodium: 600mg

Blueberry and Lemon Zest Ricotta Crepes

Prep: 20 minutes | Cook: 10 minutes | Serves: 4

Ingredients:

- 1 cup almond flour (120g)
- 1 1/2 cups skim milk (360ml)
- 2 eggs
- 1 cup part-skim ricotta cheese (245g)
- 1 cup blueberries (150g)
- 1 lemon, zested
- 2 tbsp honey (30ml)
- Cooking spray

Instructions:

1. Whisk together flour, milk, and eggs to create the crepe batter.
2. Heat a non-stick skillet and lightly coat with cooking spray. Pour batter to form thin crepes; cook until golden on both sides.
3. Mix ricotta with lemon zest and honey.
4. Fill each crepe with ricotta mixture and blueberries, fold and serve.

Nutrition Facts (Per Serving): Calories: 400 | Fat: 10g | Carbohydrates: 35g | Protein: 22g | Fiber: 4g | Sugars: 15g | Sodium: 200mg

Chia Seed And Berry Yogurt Parfait

Prep: 15 minutes (plus overnight chilling) | **Cook:** 0 minutes | **Serves:** 1

Ingredients:

- 1 cup Greek yogurt (low-fat) (245g)
- 2 tbsp chia seeds (20g)
- 1/2 cup mixed berries (raspberries, blueberries, strawberries) (75g)
- 1 tbsp honey or sugar-free sweetener (15ml)
- 1/4 cup unsweetened almond milk (60ml)

Instructions:

1. In a bowl, mix Greek yogurt with almond milk and chia seeds.
2. Add honey or sweetener to the mixture and stir well.
3. Cover the bowl and refrigerate overnight to allow chia seeds to swell.
4. Serve chilled, layered with mixed berries.

Nutrition Facts (Per Serving): Calories: 400 | Fat: 10g | Protein: 22g | Carbohydrates: 35g | Sugars: 10g | Fiber: 10g | Sodium: 85mg

Cottage Cheese And Walnut Bowl With Berries

Prep: 5 minutes | **Cook:** 0 minutes | **Serves:** 1

Ingredients:

- 1 1/3 cups cottage cheese (low-fat) (300g)
- 1/3 cup walnuts, chopped (40g)
- 2/3 cup mixed berries (raspberries, blueberries, strawberries) (100g)
- Optional: 1/2 tbsp honey or sugar-free sweetener (7.5ml)

Instructions:

1. Place the cottage cheese in a bowl.
2. Top with chopped walnuts and mixed berries.
3. Drizzle with honey or a sugar-free sweetener if desired.

Nutrition Facts (Per Serving): Calories: 400 | Fat: 24g | Protein: 32g | Carbohydrates: 24g | Sugars: 10g | Fiber: 4g

CHAPTER 4: BREAKFAST
Leisurely Weekend Brunch Ideas

Asparagus and Goat Cheese Frittata

Prep: 10 minutes | **Cook:** 20 minutes | **Serves:** 1

Ingredients:

- 6 asparagus spears, trimmed and chopped (90g)
- 4 eggs (200g)
- 2 tbsp goat cheese, crumbled (30g)
- 1 tbsp olive oil (15ml)
- Salt and pepper to taste

Instructions:

1. Preheat oven to 375°F (190°C).
2. Sauté asparagus in olive oil until tender in an oven-safe skillet.
3. Whisk eggs with salt and pepper.
4. Add goat cheese on top.
5. Cook on the stove for 3-4 minutes.
6. Bake for 15 minutes or until set.
7. Serve warm.

Nutrition Facts (Per Serving): Calories: 400 | Fat: 30g | Carbohydrates: 5g | Protein: 26g | Fiber: 2g | Sugars: 3g | Sodium: 400mg

Low-Carb Lemon Ricotta Pancakes

Prep: 10 minutes | **Cook:** 15 minutes | **Serves:** 1

Ingredients:

- 1/2 cup almond flour (50g)
- 1/4 cup ricotta cheese (62g)
- 2 eggs (100g)
- Zest of 1 lemon (2g)
- 1 tbsp honey (15ml)
- 1/2 tsp baking powder (2.5g)
- Butter for cooking

Instructions:

1. Mix almond flour, ricotta, eggs, lemon zest, lemon juice, baking powder, and honey.
2. Heat butter or oil in a skillet.
3. Pour batter to form small pancakes, cook until golden on both sides.
4. Serve warm.

Nutrition Facts (Per Serving): Calories: 400 | Fat: 32g | Carbohydrates: 10g | Protein: 20g | Fiber: 3g | Sugars: 4g | Sodium: 300mg

Grilled Tomato and Mozzarella Caprese Salad

Prep: 5 minutes | Cook: 10 minutes | Serves: 1

Ingredients:

- 2 large tomatoes, sliced (400g)
- 4 oz fresh mozzarella, sliced (113g)
- 1 tbsp olive oil (15ml)
- 1 tbsp balsamic vinegar (15ml)
- Fresh basil leaves (5g)
- Salt and pepper to taste

Instructions:

1. Grill tomato slices over medium heat for 2-3 minutes each side.
2. Arrange grilled tomatoes, mozzarella, and basil on a plate.
3. Drizzle with balsamic vinegar and olive oil.
4. Season with salt and pepper.
5. Serve immediately.

Nutrition Facts (Per Serving): Calories: 400 | Fat: 30g | Carbohydrates: 15g | Protein: 22g | Fiber: 2g | Sugars: 8g | Sodium: 400mg

Grilled Portobello Mushrooms with Poached Eggs

Prep: 10 minutes | Cook: 15 minutes | Serves: 4

Ingredients:

- 8 large portobello mushrooms (480g total)
- 8 eggs (400g total)
- 4 tbsp olive oil (60ml)
- Salt and pepper to taste
- 4 slices of whole-grain bread (280g total)
- 1/2 cup grated Parmesan cheese (60g)

Instructions:

1. Brush mushrooms with olive oil, season with salt and pepper.
2. Grill mushrooms over medium heat for 5-7 minutes each side.
3. Poach eggs in simmering water for 3-4 minutes.
4. Place poached eggs on grilled mushrooms.
5. Garnish with parsley and serve.

Nutrition Facts (Per Serving): Calories: 400 | Fat: 28g | Carbohydrates: 20g | Protein: 28g | Fiber: 4g | Sugars: 4g | Sodium: 500mg

Broccoli and Cheddar Cheese Quiche

Prep: 15 minutes | Cook: 35 minutes | Serves: 4

Ingredients:

For the crust:
- 2 cups almond flour (200g),
- 4 tbsp coconut oil (60ml),
- pinch of salt
- 2 cups chopped broccoli (180g)
- 1 cup shredded cheddar cheese (120g)
- 8 eggs (400g)
- 1 cup heavy cream (240ml)
- Salt and pepper to taste

Instructions:

1. Preheat oven to 375°F (190°C).
2. Steam broccoli until slightly tender, about 3-4 minutes. Spread evenly over pie crust.
3. Sprinkle shredded cheddar cheese over the broccoli.
4. In a mixing bowl, whisk together eggs, milk, cream, salt, pepper, and garlic powder.
5. Pour egg mixture over broccoli and cheese.
6. Bake for 35 minutes or until the quiche is set and the crust is golden brown.
7. Let the quiche cool for 10 minutes before slicing and serving.

Nutrition Facts (Per Serving): Calories: 400 | Fat: 32g | Carbohydrates: 12g | Protein: 22g | Fiber: 4g | Sugars: 3g | Sodium: 400mg

Keto-Friendly Bagels with Smoked Salmon Spread

Prep: 20 minutes | Cook: 25 minutes | Serves: 4

Ingredients:

For Bagels:
- 1 1/2 cups almond flour (150g)
- 1 tbsp baking powder (14g)
- 3 cups shredded mozzarella cheese (337.5g)
- 2 large eggs (100g)
- 4 oz cream cheese (114g)

For the spread:
- 8 oz smoked salmon (226g)
- 1/2 cup cream cheese (120g)
- 1 tbsp fresh dill, chopped (3g)
- 1 tbsp lemon juice (15ml)
- Salt to taste

Instructions:

1. Preheat oven to 400°F (200°C). Mix almond flour and baking powder.
2. Melt mozzarella and cream cheese together. Add to the flour mixture. Stir in eggs to form a dough.
3. Divide dough into 4 parts and shape each into a bagel. Place on a baking sheet lined with parchment paper.
4. Bake for 20-25 minutes until golden.
5. For the spread, mix cream cheese, smoked salmon, dill, and lemon juice.
6. Slice bagels and spread with salmon mixture.

Nutritional Facts (Per Serving): Calories: 400 | Fat: 32g | Carbohydrates: 12g | Protein: 22g | Fiber: 4g | Sugars: 3g | Sodium: 400mg

Spinach and Feta Egg Muffins

Prep: 10 minutes | Cook: 20 minutes | Serves: 4

Ingredients:

- 5 large eggs
- 1 cup chopped spinach (30g)
- 3/4 cup crumbled feta cheese (113g)
- Salt and pepper to taste
- Non-stick cooking spray

Instructions:

1. Preheat the oven to 350°F (175°C). Spray a muffin tin with non-stick spray.
2. Whisk the eggs in a bowl. Add in chopped spinach, feta cheese, salt, and pepper.
3. Pour the mixture into the muffin tins, filling each about 2/3 full.
4. Bake for 20 minutes or until the muffins are set.
5. Let them cool for a few minutes before serving.

Nutrition Facts (Per Serving): Calories: 400 | Fat: 30g | Protein: 28g | Carbohydrates: 6g | Sugars: 4g | Fiber: 2g | Sodium: 700mg

Black Bean and Corn Breakfast Quesadilla

Prep: 10 minutes | Cook: 10 minutes | Serves: 4

Ingredients:

- 4 whole-grain tortillas (200g)
- 1 cup black beans, drained and rinsed (170g)
- 1/2 cup corn kernels, fresh or frozen (thawed) (75g)
- 1 tbsp olive oil (15ml)
- 1/2 cup low-fat cheddar cheese, shredded (70g)
- 1/2 cup Greek yogurt (120ml)
- 1/4 cup salsa (60ml)
- Salt and pepper to taste

Instructions:

1. Heat olive oil in a skillet over medium heat.
2. Place a tortilla in the skillet, sprinkle with cheese, black beans, and corn. Top with another tortilla.
3. Cook until the bottom tortilla is golden brown, then flip and cook the other side.
4. Repeat with remaining tortillas and filling.
5. Serve with a dollop of Greek yogurt and salsa on top.

Nutrition Facts (Per Serving): Calories: 400 | Fat: 12g | Carbohydrates: 45g | Protein: 18g | Fiber: 8g | Sugars: 3g | Sodium: 400mg

Sundried Tomato and Goat Cheese Breakfast Flatbread

Prep: 15 minutes | Cook: 10 minutes | Serves: 4

Ingredients:

- 4 whole-grain flatbreads (200g)
- 1/2 cup sundried tomatoes, chopped (90g)
- 1 cup goat cheese, crumbled (120g)
- 1/4 cup basil leaves, chopped (6g)
- 2 tbsp olive oil (30ml)
- Salt and pepper to taste

Instructions:

1. Preheat the oven to 400°F (200°C).
2. Brush each flatbread with olive oil and sprinkle with salt and pepper.
3. Top with sundried tomatoes and goat cheese.
4. Bake for 8-10 minutes until the flatbread is crispy and the cheese is melted.
5. Garnish with fresh basil before serving.

Nutrition Facts (Per Serving): Calories: 400 | Fat: 15g | Carbohydrates: 30g | Protein: 12g | Fiber: 5g | Sugars: 4g | Sodium: 300mg

Egg White and Spinach Breakfast Burrito

Prep: 10 minutes | Cook: 5 minutes | Serves: 1

Ingredients:

- 3 egg whites (100g)
- 1 cup fresh spinach (30g)
- 1 whole-grain tortilla (60g)
- 3 tbsp shredded low-fat cheese (45g)
- 1/4 avocado, sliced (30g)
- 1 tbsp salsa (15ml)
- Salt and pepper to taste

Instructions:

1. Scramble the egg whites with spinach, salt, and pepper.
2. Warm the tortilla, then place the scrambled egg mixture in the center.
3. Top with cheese, avocado slices, and salsa.
4. Roll the tortilla to form a burrito.

Nutritional Facts (Per Serving): Calories: 400 | Fat: 15g | Carbohydrates: 35g | Protein: 25g | Fiber: 7g | Sugars: 5g | Sodium: 800mg

CHAPTER 5: BREAKFAST
Low-Carb Smoothie

Matcha Green Tea and Avocado Smoothie

Prep: 5 minutes | **Cook:** 0 minutes | **Serves:** 1

Ingredients:

- 2 tsp matcha green tea powder (4g)
- 1 whole avocado (200g)
- 1 cup unsweetened almond milk (240ml)
- 1 tbsp honey (21g)
- 2 tbsp chia seeds (28g)
- Ice cubes

Instructions:

1. Blend matcha powder, avocado, almond milk, chia seeds, honey (if using), and ice cubes until smooth.
2. Serve immediately.

Nutrition Facts (Per Serving): Calories: 400 | Fat: 30g | Carbohydrates: 28g | Protein: 8g | Fiber: 10g | Sugars: 9g | Sodium: 150mg

Mixed Berry and Flaxseed Smoothie

Prep: 5 minutes | **Cook:** 0 minutes | **Serves:** 1

Ingredients:

- 1 cup mixed berries (150g)
- 2 tbsp ground flaxseed (14g)
- 1 cup Greek yogurt, full-fat (245g)
- 1 tsp honey (7g)
- 2 tbsp almond butter (32g)
- 1 tbsp chia seeds (13g)

Instructions:

1. Combine berries, flaxseed, yogurt, honey, almond butter, and chia seeds in a blender.
2. Blend until smooth.
3. Serve chilled.

Nutrition Facts (Per Serving): Calories: 400 | Fat: 25g | Carbohydrates: 20g | Protein: 20g | Fiber: 12g | Sugars: 10g | Sodium: 70mg

Cranberry and Orange Zest Detox Smoothie

Prep: 5 minutes | Cook: 0 minutes | Serves: 1

Ingredients:

- 1/2 cup cranberries (50g) –
- 1 orange, peeled and sectioned (140g)
- 1/2 cup water (120ml)
- 1 tsp honey (7g)
- 1/2 tsp orange zest (1g)
- 1/4 cup walnuts (30g)
- 2 tbsp hemp seeds (20g)

Instructions:

1. Blend cranberries, orange, water, orange zest, walnuts, and hemp seeds, honey (if using) until smooth.
2. Serve immediately.

Nutrition Facts (Per Serving): Calories: 400 | Fat: 24g | Carbohydrates: 20g | Protein: 10g | Fiber: 6g | Sugars: 10g | Sodium: 5mg

Celery and Green Apple Hydration Smoothie

Prep: 5 minutes | Cook: 0 minutes | Serves: 1

Ingredients:

- 2 stalks celery (80g)
- 1/2 green apple, cored and sliced (90g)
- 1 cup spinach (30g)
- 1 cup coconut water (240ml) – choose a no-added-sugar variety
- 1 tbsp lemon juice (15ml)
- 1/4 cup raw almonds (30g)
- 1/2 tbsp honey (10.5g)

Instructions:

1. Combine celery, apple, spinach, coconut water, lemon juice, almonds, and honey (if using) in a blender.
2. Blend until smooth.
3. Serve immediately.

Nutrition Facts (Per Serving): Calories: 400 | Fat: 20g | Carbohydrates: 20g | Protein: 10g | Fiber: 8g | Sugars: 10g | Sodium: 250mg

CHAPTER 6: LUNCH
Salads

Turkey Bacon and Spinach Salad with Boiled Eggs

Prep: 15 minutes | Cook: 10 minutes | Serves: 1

Ingredients:

- 4 slices turkey bacon (80g)
- 2 cups spinach (60g)
- 2 large boiled eggs (100g)
- 1/4 cup cherry tomatoes, halved (37.5g)
- 1/4 avocado, sliced (30g)
- 2 tbsp olive oil (30ml)
- 1 tbsp balsamic vinegar (15ml)
- Salt and pepper to taste

Instructions:

1. Cook turkey bacon in a pan until crispy.
2. In a large bowl, mix spinach, cherry tomatoes, avocado and sliced eggs.
3. In a small bowl, whisk together olive oil, balsamic vinegar, salt, and pepper.
4. Drizzle the dressing over the salad.
5. Top with chopped turkey bacon.
6. Serve immediately.

Nutrition Facts (Per Serving): Calories: 500 | Fat: 35g | Carbohydrates: 12g | Protein: 32g | Fiber: 5g | Sugars: 4g | Sodium: 700mg

Buffalo Chicken Salad with Blue Cheese Dressing

Prep: 20 minutes | Cook: 10 minutes | Serves: 1

Ingredients:

- 1 chicken breast (200g), grilled and sliced
- 1/4 cup buffalo sauce (60ml)
- 2 cups mixed greens (60g)
- 1/4 cup carrot, shredded (30g)
- 1/4 cup celery, sliced (30g)
- 2 tbsp blue cheese dressing (30ml)
- 1 tbsp crumbled blue cheese (14g)

Instructions:

1. Season chicken breasts with salt and pepper, grill until cooked.
2. Toss grilled chicken in buffalo sauce.
3. Arrange mixed greens and cherry tomatoes on plates.
4. Top with buffalo chicken and blue cheese dressing. Sprinkle with crumbled blue cheese.

Nutritional Facts (Per Serving): Calories: 500 | Fat: 30g | Carbohydrates: 12g | Protein: 42g | Fiber: 3g | Sugars: 5g | Sodium: 800mg

Beef Fajita Salad with Avocado Lime Dressing

Prep: 20 minutes | Cook: 15 minutes | Serves: 1

Ingredients:

- 1/2 lb beef strips (225g)
- 1/2 bell pepper, sliced (60g)
- 1/2 onion, sliced (60g)
- 2 cups lettuce, shredded (100g)
- 1/4 avocado (30g) for dressing
- Juice of 1 lime (30ml)
- 2 tbsp olive oil (30ml), divided
- 1 clove garlic, minced (3g)
- Salt and pepper to taste

Instructions:

1. Sauté beef strips, bell pepper, and onion in 1 tbsp olive oil until cooked.
2. Blend avocado, lime juice, remaining olive oil, garlic, salt, and pepper to create the dressing.
3. Toss beef mixture with lettuce and drizzle with avocado lime dressing.

Nutritional Facts (Per Serving): Calories: 500 | Fat: 35g | Carbohydrates: 15g | Protein: 35g | Fiber: 5g | Sugars: 5g | Sodium: 300mg

Balsamic Glazed Portobello Mushroom Salad with Arugula

Prep: 15 minutes | Cook: 10 minutes | Serves: 1

Ingredients:

- 2 large Portobello mushrooms (240g)
- 2 cups arugula (40g)
- 1/4 cup balsamic vinegar (60ml)
- 1 tbsp olive oil (15ml)
- 1/4 cup cherry tomatoes, halved (37.5g)
- 1/4 cup shaved Parmesan cheese (30g)
- Salt and pepper to taste

Instructions:

1. Marinate mushrooms in balsamic vinegar for 10 minutes.
2. Grill mushrooms with olive oil, salt, and pepper for 5 minutes per side.
3. Toss arugula, cherry tomatoes, and grilled mushrooms. Top with Parmesan.

Nutritional Facts (Per Serving): Calories: 500 | Fat: 30g | Carbohydrates: 20g | Protein: 20g | Fiber: 4g | Sugars: 10g | Sodium: 500mg

Grilled Eggplant and Bell Pepper Salad with Feta

Prep: 20 minutes | Cook: 15 minutes | Serves: 1

Ingredients:

- 1 medium eggplant, sliced (300g)
- 1 bell pepper, sliced (120g)
- 2 tbsp olive oil (30ml)
- 1/2 cup feta cheese, crumbled (75g)
- 2 cups mixed greens (40g)
- 1 tbsp lemon juice (15ml)
- Salt and pepper to taste

Instructions:

1. Brush eggplant and bell pepper slices with olive oil, season with salt and pepper.
2. Grill vegetables until tender and slightly charred.
3. Arrange grilled vegetables on a plate.
4. Sprinkle with feta cheese and drizzle with balsamic vinegar.
5. Serve immediately.

Nutrition Facts (Per Serving): Calories: 500 | Fat: 35g | Carbohydrates: 30g | Protein: 15g | Fiber: 10g | Sugars: 15g | Sodium: 600mg

Grilled Chicken Salad with Avocado Dressing

Prep: 20 minutes | Cook: 15 minutes | Serves: 4

Ingredients:

- 2 chicken breasts (600g) –
- 8 cups mixed greens (240g)
- 2 avocados (400g)
- 1/2 cup Greek yogurt (120g)
- 4 tbsp lime juice (60ml)
- 2 tbsp olive oil (30ml)
- Salt and pepper to taste
- 1/4 cup chopped nuts (30g)
- 1/4 cup crumbled feta cheese (30g)

Instructions:

1. Preheat the grill to medium heat. Brush the chicken breasts with 1 tbsp olive oil and season with salt and pepper. Grill until cooked through, about 6-7 minutes per side. Let rest before slicing.
2. In a blender, combine avocados, Greek yogurt, lime juice, salt, and pepper. Blend until smooth for the dressing.
3. Toss the mixed greens in a large bowl with most of the avocado dressing.
4. Divide the salad among plates. Top with sliced grilled chicken, chopped nuts, and crumbled feta cheese.
5. Drizzle the remaining dressing over the chicken.

Nutrition Facts (Per Serving): Calories: 500 | Fat: 35g | Carbohydrates: 20g | Protein: 35g | Fiber: 8g | Sugars: 5g | Sodium: 300mg

Grilled Chicken and Avocado Caesar Salad

Prep: 20 minutes | Cook: 15 minutes | Serves: 2

Ingredients:

- 2 chicken breasts (300g each)
- 6 cups romaine lettuce, chopped (300g)
- 2 avocados, sliced (300g)
- 3/4 cup Caesar dressing (180ml)
- 1/2 cup Parmesan cheese, grated (60g)
- 1 1/2 cups croutons (90g)
- Salt and pepper to taste

Instructions:

1. Preheat the grill. Season chicken breasts with salt and pepper, then grill until fully cooked and nicely charred, about 6-7 minutes per side. Let them rest before slicing.
2. In a large salad bowl, combine the chopped romaine lettuce, sliced avocados, and croutons.
3. Cut the grilled chicken into strips and add to the salad.
4. Drizzle Caesar dressing over the salad and toss well to combine.
5. Sprinkle grated Parmesan cheese over the top.

Nutrition Facts (Per Serving): Calories: 500 | Fat: 35g | Carbohydrates: 20g | Protein: 35g | Fiber: 7g | Sugars: 5g | Sodium: 700mg

Salmon Nicoise Salad

Prep: 20 minutes | Cook: 15 minutes | Serves: 4

Ingredients:

- 4 salmon fillets (600g)
- 2 cups green beans, trimmed (200g)
- 1 cup olives, halved (150g)
- 2 cups new potatoes, quartered (300g)
- 8 cups mixed salad greens (200g)
- 1/4 cup Dijon mustard dressing (60ml)
- Salt and pepper to taste

Instructions:

1. Season salmon with salt and pepper, grill until cooked through, set aside.
2. potatoes until tender, blanch green beans.
3. Arrange salad greens, potatoes, green beans, olives, and salmon.
4. Drizzle with Dijon mustard dressing.

Nutrition Facts (Per Serving): Calories: 500 | Fat: 20g | Carbohydrates: 30g | Protein: 40g | Fiber: 5g | Sugars: 5g | Sodium: 400mg

Southwest Steak Salad

Prep: 15 minutes | Cook: 10 minutes | Serves: 4

Ingredients:

- 1 lb flank steak (450g)
- 1 can black beans, rinsed (15 oz or 425g)
- 1 cup corn kernels (150g)
- Salt and pepper to taste
- 1 cup diced tomatoes (180g)
- 8 cups romaine lettuce, chopped (400g)
- 1/4 cup spicy ranch dressing (60ml)

Instructions:

1. Season steak with salt and pepper. Grill over medium-high heat for 5 minutes per side. Let rest, then slice thinly.
2. Toss lettuce with black beans, corn, and tomatoes.
3. Top with steak slices and drizzle with spicy ranch dressing.

Nutrition Facts (Per Serving): Calories: 500 | Fat: 20g | Carbohydrates: 30g | Protein: 45g | Fiber: 8g | Sugars: 5g | Sodium: 500mg

Kale, Apple, and Roasted Almond Salad with Feta

Prep: 15 minutes | Cook: 0 minutes | Serves: 1

Ingredients:

- 2 cups kale, chopped (134g)
- 1/2 medium apple, diced (91g)
- 1/4 cup roasted almonds, chopped (30g)
- 1/4 cup feta cheese, crumbled (30g)
- 2 tbsp olive oil (30ml)
- 1 tbsp apple cider vinegar (15ml)
- 1/2 tsp honey (3.5g)
- Salt and pepper to taste

Instructions:

1. Toss kale, half an apple, almonds, and feta cheese in a salad bowl.
2. Whisk together olive oil, apple cider vinegar, reduced honey, salt, and pepper to create the dressing.
3. Drizzle the dressing over the salad and toss to combine.

Nutritional Facts (Per Serving): Calories: 500 | Fat: 35g | Carbohydrates: 22g | Protein: 12g | Fiber: 6g | Sugars: 10g | Sodium: 500mg

Cobb Salad with Turkey Bacon

Prep: 15 minutes | Cook: 10 minutes | Serves: 4

Ingredients:

- 2 chicken breasts, grilled and diced (400g)
- 8 slices turkey bacon, cooked and chopped (240g)
- 4 hard-boiled eggs, sliced
- 2 avocados, diced (300g)
- 1/2 cup blue cheese, crumbled (60g)
- 8 cups mixed salad greens (400g)
- 1/4 cup Greek yogurt dressing (60ml)
- Salt and pepper to taste

Instructions:

1. Arrange salad greens in bowls.
2. Top with chicken, turkey bacon, eggs, avocados, and blue cheese.
3. Drizzle with Greek yogurt dressing.

Nutrition Facts (Per Serving): Calories: 500 | Fat: 30g | Carbohydrates: 15g | Protein: 40g | Fiber: 8g | Sugars: 5g | Sodium: 500mg

Caprese Salad with Grilled Chicken

Prep: 15 minutes | Cook: 10 minutes | Serves: 4

Ingredients:

- 2 large ripe tomatoes, sliced (400g)
- 8 oz fresh mozzarella, sliced (225g)
- 1/4 cup fresh basil leaves (15g)
- 4 chicken breasts, grilled and sliced (800g)
- 2 tbsp balsamic glaze (30ml)
- Salt and pepper to taste

Instructions:

1. Layer tomato, mozzarella, basil, and grilled chicken on a plate.
2. Drizzle with balsamic glaze.
3. Season with salt and pepper.

Nutrition Facts (Per Serving): Calories: 500 | Fat: 20g | Carbohydrates: 15g | Protein: 60g | Fiber: 2g | Sugars: 8g | Sodium: 300mg

CHAPTER 7: LUNCH
Hearty Soups and Stews

Hearty Vegetable and Bean Soup

Prep: 10 minutes | Cook: 30 minutes | Serves: 4

Ingredients:

- 1 onion, chopped (150g)
- 2 carrots, chopped (120g)
- 2 celery stalks, chopped (80g)
- 2 garlic cloves, minced (6g)
- 1 can diced tomatoes (400g)
- 1 can kidney beans, drained and rinsed (400g)
- 4 cups vegetable broth (960ml)
- 1 tsp dried thyme (1g)
- 1 tsp dried basil (1g)
- 2 cups spinach, chopped (60g)
- 1/4 cup olive oil (60ml)
- 1 cup tofu, cubed (150g)
- Salt and pepper to taste

Instructions:

1. In a large pot, heat olive oil over medium heat. Sauté onion, carrots, celery, and garlic until softened.
2. Add diced tomatoes, kidney beans, vegetable broth, thyme, basil, and tofu. Bring to a boil.
3. Reduce heat and simmer for 20 minutes. Stir in spinach and cook until wilted.
4. Season with salt and pepper. Serve hot.

Nutrition Facts (Per Serving): Calories: 500 | Fat: 20g | Carbohydrates: 30g | Protein: 25g | Fiber: 10g | Sugars: 9g | Sodium: 500mg

Tomato and Basil Bisque with Almond Milk

Prep: 10 minutes | Cook: 20 minutes | Serves: 4

Ingredients:

- 1 onion, chopped (150g)
- 2 garlic cloves, minced (6g)
- 1 can crushed tomatoes (800g)
- 2 cups almond milk (480ml)
- 1 tbsp fresh basil, chopped (3g)
- 1/4 cup olive oil (60ml)
- 1/2 cup pine nuts (70g)
- Salt and pepper to taste

Instructions:

1. Heat olive oil in a pot, sauté onion and garlic until translucent.
2. Add crushed tomatoes and bring to a simmer.
3. Add almond milk and basil, continue to simmer for 15 minutes.
4. Use an immersion blender to puree the soup until smooth.
5. Toast pine nuts in a dry skillet until golden and sprinkle on top of the soup before serving.
6. Season with salt and pepper. Serve warm.

Nutritional Facts (Per Serving): Calories: 500 | Fat: 35g | Carbohydrates: 25g | Protein: 10g | Fiber: 6g | Sugars: 10g | Sodium: 300mg

Chicken and Spinach Soup with Fresh Herbs

Prep: 15 minutes | Cook: 30 minutes | Serves: 4

Ingredients:

- 4 chicken breasts, diced (800g)
- 1 onion, chopped (150g)
- 2 carrots, chopped (120g)
- 4 garlic cloves, minced (12g)
- 6 cups chicken broth (1440ml)
- 4 cups spinach, chopped (120g)
- 2 tbsp olive oil (30ml)
- 2 tbsp fresh parsley, chopped (6g)
- 2 tbsp fresh dill, chopped (6g)
- 1/4 cup heavy cream (60ml)
- 1/4 cup grated Parmesan cheese (30g)
- Salt and pepper to taste

Instructions:

1. Heat olive oil in a pot and cook chicken, onion, carrots, and garlic until the chicken is cooked through.
2. Add chicken broth and bring to a boil. Reduce heat and simmer for 20 minutes.
3. Add spinach, parsley, and dill. Cook for an additional 5 minutes.
4. Stir in heavy cream and Parmesan cheese until well combined.
5. Season with salt and pepper.

Nutrition Facts (Per Serving): Calories: 500 | Fat: 35g | Carbohydrates: 15g | Protein: 40g | Fiber: 4g | Sugars: 5g | Sodium: 500mg

Turkey and White Bean Chili

Prep: 15 minutes | Cook: 30 minutes | Serves: 4

Ingredients:

- 1.5 lbs ground turkey (675g)
- 1 large onion, chopped (150g)
- 4 cloves garlic, minced (12g)
- 2 cans white beans, drained and rinsed (800g)
- 1 can diced tomatoes, no added sugar (400g)
- 3 cups chicken broth (720ml)
- 1 tbsp olive oil (15ml)
- 2 tsp cumin (4.6g)
- 2 tsp chili powder (5g)
- 1 tsp paprika (2.5g)
- Salt and pepper to taste
- 1/4 cup sour cream (for topping) (60ml)
- 1/4 cup shredded cheese (for topping) (30g)
- Chopped cilantro (optional for topping)

Instructions:

1. Heat the olive oil in a large pot over medium heat. Add the ground turkey, onion, and garlic. Cook until the turkey is browned.
2. Stir in the white beans, diced tomatoes, chicken broth, cumin, chili powder, paprika, salt, and pepper.
3. Bring the mixture to a boil, then reduce heat and simmer for 20-25 minutes, allowing the flavors to meld.
4. Serve the chili hot, garnished with sour cream, shredded cheese, and chopped cilantro if desired.

Nutrition Facts (Per Serving): Calories: 500 | Fat: 35g | Carbohydrates: 30g | Protein: 35g | Fiber: 10g | Sugars: 5g | Sodium: 600mg

Greek-Style Lemon and Olive Chicken Stew

Prep: 15 minutes | Cook: 30 minutes | Serves: 4

Ingredients:

- 4 chicken thighs, bone-in, skin-on (1200g)
- Juice and zest of 2 lemons
- 1 large onion, chopped (150g)
- 4 cloves garlic, minced (12g)
- 3 cups chicken broth (720ml)
- 2 tbsp olive oil (30ml)
- 1 tsp dried oregano (1g)
- Salt and pepper to taste
- 1 cup pitted Kalamata olives (150g)
- 1/2 cup feta cheese, crumbled (75g)

Instructions:

1. Heat olive oil in a large pot over medium heat. Brown the chicken thighs on both sides.
2. Remove the chicken and sauté the onion and garlic in the same pot until translucent.
3. Add lemon juice, zest, olives, chicken broth, oregano, salt, and pepper. Bring to a simmer.
4. Return the chicken to the pot, cover, and simmer for 30 minutes.
5. Sprinkle feta cheese over the stew before serving.

Nutrition Facts (Per Serving): Calories: 500 | Fat: 35g | Carbohydrates: 15g | Protein: 38g | Fiber: 3g | Sugars: 5g | Sodium: 800mg

Hearty Turkey and Vegetable Stew

Prep: 15 minutes | Cook: 45 minutes | Serves: 4

Ingredients:

- 1.5 lbs ground turkey (675g)
- 2 carrots, diced (120g)
- 2 celery stalks, diced (80g)
- 1 large onion, diced (150g)
- 4 cups beef broth (960ml)
- 1 can diced tomatoes, no added sugar (400g)
- 2 tbsp olive oil (30ml)
- 1 tsp thyme (1g)
- Salt and pepper to taste
- 1/4 cup heavy cream (60ml)
- 1/4 cup grated Parmesan cheese (30g)

Instructions:

1. In a large pot, heat 1 tbsp olive oil and cook ground turkey until browned.
2. Remove turkey and set aside. In the same pot, add another 1 tbsp of olive oil, and cook carrots, celery, and onion until vegetables are soft.
3. Return the turkey to the pot. Add beef broth, diced tomatoes, thyme, salt, and pepper. Bring to a boil.
4. Reduce heat and simmer for 30 minutes.
5. Stir in heavy cream and Parmesan cheese until well combined.
6. Adjust seasoning and serve the stew hot.

Nutrition Facts (Per Serving): Calories: 500 | Fat: 35g | Carbohydrates: 20g | Protein: 38g | Fiber: 5g | Sugars: 8g | Sodium: 800mg

Spicy Chicken and Tomato Stew

Prep: 10 minutes | Cook: 30 minutes | Serves: 4

Ingredients:

- 1.5 lbs chicken thighs, boneless, skinless (675g)
- 1 can diced tomatoes, no added sugar (400g)
- 1 large onion, chopped (150g)
- 4 cloves garlic, minced (12g)
- 1 red bell pepper, diced (150g)
- 2 tsp chili powder (4g)
- 1 tsp cumin (2.3g)
- 2 cups chicken broth (480ml)
- 2 tbsp olive oil (30ml)
- Salt and pepper to taste
- 1/4 cup sour cream (60ml) – for serving
- 1/4 cup shredded cheddar cheese (30g) – for serving

Instructions:

1. Heat 1 tbsp olive oil in a large pot. Add chicken and cook until browned. Remove and set aside.
2. Add the remaining olive oil to the pot and sauté onion, garlic, and bell pepper until soft.
3. Stir in chili powder and cumin, cooking for another minute. Add diced tomatoes and chicken broth. Bring to a boil.
4. Return chicken to the pot, reduce heat to low, and simmer for 30 minutes. Season with salt and pepper.
5. Serve hot, topped with sour cream and shredded cheddar cheese.

Nutrition Facts (Per Serving): Calories: 500 | Fat: 35g | Carbohydrates: 20g | Protein: 38g | Fiber: 5g | Sugars: 8g | Sodium: 700mg

Pork, Cabbage, and Apple Stew

Prep: 15 minutes | Cook: 1 hour | Serves: 4

Ingredients:

- 1.5 lbs pork shoulder, cut into cubes (675g)
- 4 cups cabbage, chopped (400g)
- 1 large apple, diced (150g)
- 1 onion, chopped (150g)
- 2 cups chicken broth (480ml)
- Salt and pepper to taste
- 1 tbsp apple cider vinegar (15ml)
- 1 tsp thyme (1g)
- 2 tbsp olive oil (30ml)
- 1/4 cup heavy cream (60ml)
- 2 tbsp almond flour (15g)

Instructions:

1. Heat 1 tbsp olive oil in a large pot. Add pork cubes and brown on all sides. Remove and set aside.
2. In the same pot, add the remaining olive oil and sauté onion until translucent.
3. Add cabbage, diced apple, thyme, apple cider vinegar, and chicken broth. Bring to a boil.
4. Return the pork to the pot, reduce heat to low, and simmer for about 45 minutes, or until the pork is tender. Season the stew with salt and pepper.
6. Serve hot with a dollop of sour cream on top of each serving.

Nutrition Facts (Per Serving): Calories: 500 | Fat: 35g | Carbohydrates: 20g | Protein: 30g | Fiber: 5g | Sugars: 10g | Sodium: 500mg

Ratatouille: Mixed Vegetable Stew

Prep: 20 minutes | **Cook:** 40 minutes | **Serves:** 4

Ingredients:

- 1 lb pork loin, diced (450g)
- 1 eggplant, diced (300g)
- 1 zucchini, diced (150g)
- 1 red bell pepper, diced (150g)
- 1 onion, chopped (150g)
- 1 tomato, chopped (100g)
- 3 cloves garlic, minced
- 3 tbsp olive oil (45ml)
- 1 tsp thyme (1g)
- 1 tsp rosemary (1g)
- Salt and pepper to taste
- 1/4 cup grated Parmesan cheese (30g)

Instructions:

1. Heat 1 tbsp olive oil in a large pot. Brown the diced pork, then remove and set aside.
2. In the same pot, add 1 tbsp olive oil and sauté eggplant until soft. Remove and set aside.
3. Add the remaining olive oil, sauté zucchini, bell pepper, and onion.
4. Add garlic, tomato, thyme, rosemary, salt, and pepper. Cook for 10 minutes.
5. Return pork and eggplant to the pot. Simmer for 30 minutes.
6. Adjust seasoning. Sprinkle with Parmesan cheese before serving.

Nutrition Facts (Per Serving): Calories: 500 | Fat: 35g | Carbohydrates: 20g | Protein: 30g | Fiber: 6g | Sugars: 8g | Sodium: 500mg

Moroccan-Spiced Chickpea and Eggplant Stew

Prep: 15 minutes | **Cook:** 40 minutes | **Serves:** 4

Ingredients:

- 1 large eggplant, cubed (400g)
- 2 cans chickpeas, drained and rinsed (800g)
- 1 large onion, chopped (150g)
- 4 cloves garlic, minced (12g)
- 1 can diced tomatoes (400g)
- 3 cups vegetable broth (720ml)
- 1 tsp cumin (2.3g)
- 1 tsp paprika (2.5g)
- 1/2 tsp cinnamon (1.3g)
- 2 tbsp olive oil (30ml)
- Salt and pepper to taste
- 1/4 cup almonds, chopped (30g)
- 2 tbsp raisins (30g)

Instructions:

1. Heat olive oil in a large pot. Sauté onion and garlic until translucent.
2. Add eggplant, chickpeas, cumin, paprika, and cinnamon. Cook for 5 minutes.
3. Stir in diced tomatoes and vegetable broth. Bring to a boil.
4. Reduce heat and simmer for 35 minutes.
5. Add almonds and raisins in the last 5 minutes of cooking. Season with salt and pepper.

Nutrition Facts (Per Serving): Calories: 500 | Fat: 20g | Carbohydrates: 30g | Protein: 20g | Fiber: 15g | Sugars: 10g | Sodium: 800mg

Beef and Green Bean Stew

Prep: 15 minutes | Cook: 1 hour | Serves: 4

Ingredients:

- 1.5 lbs beef stew meat, cubed (675g)
- 3 cups green beans, trimmed (300g)
- 1 large onion, chopped (150g)
- 4 cloves garlic, minced (12g)
- 4 cups beef broth (960ml)
- 2 tbsp tomato paste (30g)
- 2 tbsp olive oil (30ml)
- 1/4 cup heavy cream (60ml)
- Salt and pepper to taste
- 2 tbsp almond flour (15g)

Instructions:

1. Heat 1 tbsp olive oil in a pot and brown beef on all sides. Remove beef and set aside.
2. In the same pot, add the remaining olive oil, onion, and garlic. Cook until softened.
3. Return beef to the pot. Stir in tomato paste, beef broth, green beans, and almond flour.
4. Bring to a boil, then reduce heat and simmer for 45 minutes to an hour, until beef is tender.
5. Stir in heavy cream and cook for an additional 5 minutes.
6. Season with salt and pepper.

Nutrition Facts (Per Serving): Calories: 500 | Fat: 35g | Carbohydrates: 15g | Protein: 40g | Fiber: 4g | Sugars: 5g | Sodium: 800mg

Beef and Mushroom Stew

Prep: 15 minutes | Cook: 30 minutes | Serves: 4

Ingredients:

- 1.5 lbs beef stew meat, cut into 1-inch cubes (675g)
- 3 cups mushrooms, sliced (225g)
- 1 large onion, chopped (200g)
- 4 garlic cloves, minced (12g)
- 4 cups beef broth (960ml)
- 2 tbsp Worcestershire sauce (30ml)
- 2 tbsp olive oil (30ml)
- 1 tsp thyme (1g)
- Salt and pepper to taste
- 1/4 cup heavy cream (60ml)
- 1/4 cup grated Parmesan cheese (30g)

Instructions:

1. Brown beef in 1 tbsp olive oil for 5-7 minutes, then set aside.
2. Sauté onions and garlic in the same pot for 2-3 minutes.
3. Add mushrooms and cook until browned, about 5 minutes.
4. Return beef, add broth, Worcestershire, thyme, salt, and pepper. Bring to a boil.
5. Simmer for 20-25 minutes until tender, then stir in cream and cook 5 more minutes.
6. Adjust seasoning and serve with Parmesan.

Nutrition Facts (Per Serving): Calories: 500 | Fat: 35g | Carbohydrates: 15g | Protein: 38g | Fiber: 2g | Sugars: 5g | Sodium: 800mg

CHAPTER 8: LUNCH
Poultry and Meat Dish

Roasted Chicken with Mediterranean Vegetables

Prep: 15 minutes | Cook: 25 minutes | Serves: 4

Ingredients:

- 4 chicken breasts (800g)
- 2 zucchinis, sliced (400g)
- 1 bell pepper, chopped (150g)
- 1 cup cherry tomatoes (150g)
- Salt and pepper to taste
- 2 tbsp olive oil (30ml)
- 2 garlic cloves, minced (6g)
- 1 tsp thyme (1g)
- 1 tsp rosemary (1g)

Instructions:

1. Preheat the oven to 400°F (200°C).
2. In a large bowl, combine zucchini, bell pepper, cherry tomatoes, olive oil, garlic, thyme, and rosemary.
3. Place the chicken breasts on a baking sheet, season with salt and pepper, and surround them with the vegetable mixture.
4. Roast in the oven for 25 minutes, or until chicken is cooked through and vegetables are tender.

Nutrition Facts (Per Serving): Calories: 500 | Fat: 22g | Carbohydrates: 15g | Protein: 65g | Fiber: 5g | Sugars: 5g | Sodium: 300mg

Lemon Herb Grilled Lamb Chops with Asparagus

Prep: 15 minutes (plus marinating time) | Cook: 10 minutes | Serves: 4

Ingredients:

- 8 lamb chops (800g)
- 2 tbsp olive oil (30ml)
- 2 lemons, juiced (100ml)
- 2 tbsp fresh rosemary, chopped (6g)
- 2 tbsp fresh thyme, chopped (6g)
- 1 lb asparagus, ends trimmed (450g)
- Salt and pepper to taste

Instructions:

1. Marinate lamb chops with lemon juice, olive oil, rosemary, thyme, salt, and pepper for at least 1 hour in the refrigerator.
2. Preheat grill to medium-high heat.
3. Grill lamb chops for about 4-5 minutes per side or until desired doneness.
4. Steam or grill asparagus until tender, about 5-6 minutes. Serve lamb chops with asparagus.

Nutrition Facts (Per Serving): Calories: 500 | Fat: 35g | Carbohydrates: 10g | Protein: 40g | Fiber: 3g | Sugars: 4g | Sodium: 200mg

Cauliflower Shepherd's Pie

Prep: 20 minutes | **Cook:** 35 minutes | **Serves:** 4

Ingredients:

- 1 lb lean ground turkey (450g)
- 1 medium onion, chopped (110g)
- 2 carrots, peeled and diced (120g)
- 1 cup peas (145g)
- 2 cups cauliflower florets (200g)
- 1/4 cup chicken broth (60ml)
- 2 tbsp tomato paste (30ml)
- 1 tbsp olive oil (15ml)
- 1/4 cup Greek yogurt (60g)
- Salt and pepper to taste

Instructions:

1. Preheat the oven to 375°F (190°C).
2. In a skillet, heat olive oil over medium heat. Add turkey, onions, and carrots, and cook until meat is browned.
3. Stir in peas, tomato paste, and chicken broth. Simmer for 10 minutes. Season with salt and pepper.
4. Steam cauliflower florets until tender, then mash with Greek yogurt until smooth.
5. In a baking dish, layer the meat mixture, then top with cauliflower mash.
6. Bake for 20 minutes, until the top is slightly browned.

Nutrition Facts (Per Serving): Calories: 500 | Fat: 22g | Carbohydrates: 30g | Protein: 35g | Fiber: 8g | Sugars: 10g | Sodium: 500mg

Meatloaf with Ground Chicken and Spinach

Prep: 15 minutes | **Cook:** 1 hour | **Serves:** 4

Ingredients:

- 1.5 lbs ground chicken (675g)
- 3 cups spinach, chopped (90g)
- 1 large onion, chopped (200g)
- 2 eggs (100g)
- 1/4 cup almond flour (30g)
- 2 tbsp tomato paste (30ml)
- 1 tsp garlic powder (2.8g)
- Salt and pepper to taste
- 1/4 cup grated Parmesan cheese (30g)
- 1 tbsp olive oil (15ml)

Instructions:

1. Preheat the oven to 375°F (190°C). Grease a loaf pan with olive oil.
2. In a large bowl, mix together ground chicken, spinach, onion, eggs, almond flour, tomato paste, garlic powder, salt, and pepper.
3. Transfer the mixture to the prepared loaf pan, pressing it down evenly.
4. Sprinkle grated Parmesan cheese on top.
5. Bake in the preheated oven for about 1 hour or until the meatloaf is cooked through.
6. Remove from the oven and let it rest for 10 minutes before slicing.

Nutrition Facts (Per Serving): Calories: 500 | Fat: 30g | Carbohydrates: 10g | Protein: 50g | Fiber: 3g | Sugars: 2g | Sodium: 400mg

Chicken Tikka Masala with Basmati Rice

Prep: 20 minutes | Cook: 30 minutes | Serves: 4

Ingredients:

- 1 lb chicken breast, cubed (450g)
- 1 cup basmati rice (200g)
- 1 onion, chopped (150g)
- 2 garlic cloves, minced (6g)
- 1 tbsp olive oil (15ml)
- 1 can low-sugar tomato sauce (400g)
- 2 tbsp garam masala (12g)
- 1 tsp turmeric (3g)
- 1/2 cup Greek yogurt (120g)
- Salt and pepper to taste

Instructions:

1. Cook basmati rice according to package instructions.
2. In a pan, heat olive oil and sauté onion and garlic until translucent.
3. Add chicken and cook until browned.
4. Stir in garam masala, turmeric, tomato sauce, and season with salt and pepper. Simmer for 20 minutes.
5. Stir in Greek yogurt and cook for another 5 minutes.
6. Serve chicken tikka masala over basmati rice.

Nutrition Facts (Per Serving): Calories: 500 | Fat: 12g | Carbohydrates: 50g | Protein: 45g | Fiber: 4g | Sugars: 8g | Sodium: 300mg

Beef and Eggplant Casserole

Prep: 20 minutes | Cook: 1 hour | Serves: 6

Ingredients:

- 1.5 lbs ground beef (675g)
- 1 large eggplant, sliced (500g)
- 1 large onion, chopped (150g)
- 4 cloves garlic, minced (12g)
- 1 can crushed tomatoes (400g)
- Salt and pepper to taste
- 1.5 cups shredded mozzarella cheese (150g)
- 3 tbsp olive oil (45ml)
- 1 tsp dried basil (1g)
- 1 tsp dried oregano (1g)

Instructions:

1. Preheat the oven to 375°F (190°C).
2. Heat 1 tbsp olive oil in a skillet and cook ground beef, onion, and garlic until the beef is browned.
3. Layer half of the sliced eggplant in a baking dish.
4. Top with half of the cooked beef mixture and half of the crushed tomatoes.
5. Repeat the layers with the remaining eggplant, beef mixture, and tomatoes.
6. Sprinkle with basil, oregano, salt, and pepper.
7. Drizzle the remaining olive oil over the top.
8. Cover with shredded mozzarella cheese.
9. Bake for 45 minutes until the eggplant is tender and the cheese is golden brown.

Nutrition Facts (Per Serving): Calories: 500 | Fat: 35g | Carbohydrates: 20g | Protein: 35g | Fiber: 6g | Sugars: 10g | Sodium: 500mg

Vegetable and Lentil Curry with Brown Rice

Prep: 15 minutes | Cook: 40 minutes | Serves: 4

Ingredients:

- 1 cup brown rice (195g)
- 1 tbsp olive oil (15ml)
- 1 onion, chopped (110g)
- 2 garlic cloves, minced (6g)
- 1 carrot, diced (60g)
- 1 zucchini, diced (200g)
- 1 tbsp curry powder (6g)
- 1 bell pepper, chopped (150g)
- 1 cup lentils (200g)
- 2 cups vegetable broth (480ml)
- 1 can diced tomatoes (400g)
- Salt and pepper to taste

Instructions:

1. Cook brown rice according to package instructions.
2. In a large pot, heat olive oil over medium heat. Add onion and garlic, sauté until translucent.
3. Add carrot, zucchini, bell pepper, lentils, vegetable broth, diced tomatoes, and curry powder. Stir well.
4. Bring to a boil, then reduce heat and simmer for 30 minutes, or until lentils are tender.
5. Serve the curry over a portion of brown rice.

Nutrition Facts (Per Serving): Calories: 500 | Fat: 10g | Carbohydrates: 80g | Protein: 20g | Fiber: 15g | Sugars: 8g | Sodium: 400mg

Zucchini Noodles with Turkey Meatballs in a Low-Sugar Marinara Sauce

Prep: 20 minutes | Cook: 30 minutes | Serves: 4

Ingredients:

- 1 lb ground turkey (450g)
- 4 zucchinis, spiralized (800g)
- 1 cup low-sugar marinara sauce (240ml)
- 1 egg (50g)
- 1/4 cup almond flour (25g)
- 1/4 cup grated Parmesan cheese (30g)
- 2 tbsp olive oil (30ml)
- 1 tsp garlic powder (3g)
- 1 tsp onion powder (3g)
- Salt and pepper to taste

Instructions:

1. Preheat oven to 180°C (350°F).
2. In a bowl, mix the ground turkey, egg, almond flour, parmesan, garlic powder, oregano, salt, and pepper. Form into small meatballs.
3. Place meatballs on a baking sheet and bake for 15-20 minutes until cooked through.
4. While the meatballs are baking, heat the marinara sauce in a pan over low heat.
5. In another pan, lightly sauté the zucchini noodles for 2-3 minutes until tender.
6. Once the meatballs are done, add them to the marinara sauce and simmer for 5 minutes.

Nutrition Facts (Per Serving): Calories: 500 | Fat: 28g | Carbohydrates: 18g | Protein: 45g | Fiber: 4g | Sugars: 8g | Sodium: 500mg

Beef and Vegetable Kabobs with a Side of Greek Yogurt Tzatziki

Prep: 25 minutes | Cook: 10 minutes | Serves: 4

Ingredients:

- 1 lb lean beef, cubed (450g)
- 2 bell peppers, cut into pieces (300g)
- 2 zucchinis, cut into pieces (400g)
- 1 red onion, cut into chunks (150g)
- 2 tbsp olive oil (30ml)
- 1 tsp dried oregano (1g)
- Salt and pepper to taste
- 1 cup Greek yogurt (245g)
- 1 cucumber, grated and drained (150g)
- 1 tbsp lemon juice (15ml)
- 2 garlic cloves, minced (6g)
- 1 tbsp dill, chopped (3g)

Instructions:

1. Preheat the grill to medium-high heat.
2. Thread beef, bell peppers, zucchinis, and red onion onto skewers. Brush with olive oil and season with oregano, salt, and pepper.
3. Grill kabobs, turning occasionally, until beef reaches desired doneness, about 10 minutes.
4. For the tzatziki, combine Greek yogurt, cucumber, lemon juice, garlic, and dill. Season with salt and pepper.
5. Serve kabobs with tzatziki sauce on the side.

Nutrition Facts (Per Serving): Calories: 500 | Fat: 28g | Carbohydrates: 15g | Protein: 45g | Fiber: 3g | Sugars: 9g | Sodium: 400mg

Herb-Roasted Pork Loin with Apples and Parsnips

Prep: 15 minutes | Cook: 1 hour | Serves: 4

Ingredients:

- 2 lb pork loin (900g)
- 2 apples, sliced (360g)
- 2 parsnips, sliced (250g)
- 2 tbsp olive oil (30ml)
- 1 tsp rosemary (1g)
- 1 tsp thyme (1g)
- 1 tsp sage (1g)
- Salt and pepper to taste

Instructions:

1. Preheat the oven to 375°F (190°C).
2. Season the pork loin with rosemary, thyme, sage, salt, and pepper.
3. In a roasting pan, place the pork loin and surround it with sliced apples and parsnips. Drizzle with olive oil.
4. Roast in the oven for about 1 hour, or until the pork loin reaches an internal temperature of 145°F (63°C).
5. Let the pork rest for 10 minutes before slicing.

Nutrition Facts (Per Serving): Calories: 500 | Fat: 22g | Carbohydrates: 30g | Protein: 45g | Fiber: 5g | Sugars: 15g | Sodium: 300mg

Steak Fajita Bowls with Cilantro Lime Rice

Prep: 20 minutes | Cook: 20 minutes | Serves: 4

Ingredients:

- 1 lb lean steak, sliced (450g)
- 2 bell peppers, sliced (300g)
- 1 onion, sliced (150g)
- 2 tbsp olive oil (30ml)
- 1 tsp cumin (2g)
- 1 tsp paprika (2g)
- 1 cup brown rice (195g)
- 2 tbsp lime juice (30ml)
- 1/4 cup chopped cilantro (15g)
- 1/2 cup Greek yogurt (120g)
- Salt and pepper to taste

Instructions:

1. Cook brown rice with lime juice and cilantro according to package instructions.

In a pan, heat 1 tbsp olive oil and cook steak until browned. Set aside.

In the same pan, add remaining olive oil, bell peppers, and onion. Sauté until soft.

Mix steak with vegetables and season with cumin, paprika, salt, and pepper.

Serve steak fajita mixture over cilantro lime rice with a dollop of Greek yogurt on top.

Nutrition Facts (Per Serving): Calories: 500 | Fat: 22g | Carbohydrates: 35g | Protein: 40g | Fiber: 5g | Sugars: 6g | Sodium: 300mg

Stuffed Bell Peppers with Ground Turkey and Quinoa

Prep: 20 minutes | Cook: 40 minutes | Serves: 4

Ingredients:

- 4 bell peppers, halved and seeded (480g)
- 1.5 lbs ground turkey (675g)
- 1 cup cooked quinoa (185g)
- 1 large onion, chopped (150g)
- 4 cloves garlic, minced (12g)
- 1 can diced tomatoes, drained (400g)
- 1 tbsp cumin (4.6g)
- 1 tbsp paprika (5g)
- 2 tbsp olive oil (30ml)
- Salt and pepper to taste
- 1/4 cup grated Parmesan cheese (30g) – for topping

Instructions:

1. Preheat oven to 375°F (190°C).
2. Cook 1 lb ground turkey in 1 tbsp olive oil until browned.
3. Add 1 chopped onion and 2 minced garlic cloves; sauté until soft.
4. Mix in 1 cup cooked quinoa, 1 can diced tomatoes, 1 tsp cumin, 1 tsp paprika, salt, and pepper; cook 5 min.
5. Stuff mix into 4 halved bell peppers, place in a dish, drizzle with oil.
6. Cover, bake 30 min. Uncover, top with 1/4 cup Parmesan, bake 10 min.

Nutrition Facts (Per Serving): Calories: 500 | Fat: 25g | Carbohydrates: 30g | Protein: 40g | Fiber: 6g | Sugars: 8g | Sodium: 500mg

CHAPTER 9: SNACK
Healthy Snack Options

Almond and Chia Seed Energy Balls

Prep: 15 minutes | No Cook | Serves: 10

Ingredients:

- 1/2 cup almonds (71.5g)
- 2 tbsp chia seeds (20g)
- 1/4 cup rolled oats (22.5g)
- 2 tbsp honey (30ml)
- 1/4 cup almond butter (65g)
- 1/2 tsp vanilla extract (2.5ml)
- Pinch of salt

Instructions:

1. In a food processor, pulse almonds, oats, and chia seeds until coarsely ground.
2. Add honey, almond butter, vanilla extract, and a pinch of salt to the food processor. Pulse until the mixture becomes sticky and holds together when pinched.
3. Take small portions of the mixture and roll into balls, each about the size of a cherry.
4. Place the energy balls on a baking sheet or plate and refrigerate for at least 1 hour to set.
5. Enjoy one energy ball as a serving.

Nutrition Facts (Per Serving): Calories: 220 | Fat: 15g | Carbohydrates: 18g | Protein: 6g | Fiber: 4g | Sugars: 9g | Sodium: 10mg

Avocado and Lime Mousse

Prep: 15 minutes | No Cook | Serves: 4

Ingredients:

- 2 ripe avocados (400g)
- Juice and zest of 2 limes (60ml juice)
- 1,5 tbsp honey (30g)
- 1/2 cup heavy cream (120ml)
- 1 tsp vanilla extract (5ml)

Instructions:

1. In a blender, combine avocados, lime juice, lime zest, honey, and vanilla extract. Blend until smooth.
2. In a separate bowl, whip the heavy cream until stiff peaks form.
3. Gently fold the whipped cream into the avocado mixture.
4. Divide the mousse into serving dishes and refrigerate for at least 1 hour before serving.

Nutritional Facts (Per Serving): Calories: 220 | Fat: 18g | Carbohydrates: 18g | Protein: 2g | Fiber: 6g | Sugars: 5g | Sodium: 10mg

Avocado and Cottage Cheese Dip

Prep: 10 minutes | No Cook | Serves: 4

Ingredients:

- 2 ripe avocados (200g each)
- 1 cup cottage cheese (226g)
- Juice of 1 lime (30ml)
- 2 tbsp chopped cilantro (30g)
- 1/4 tsp garlic powder (1g)
- Salt and pepper to taste)

Instructions:

1. Scoop out the avocado flesh into a mixing bowl and mash it until smooth.
2. Add the cottage cheese, lime juice, cilantro, garlic powder, salt, and pepper to the mashed avocado.
3. Mix all the ingredients together until well combined and creamy.
4. Adjust the seasoning as needed.
5. Chill the dip for about 30 minutes before serving to enhance the flavors.
6. Serve the dip with sliced vegetables or whole grain crackers for dipping.

Nutrition Facts (Per Serving): Calories: 220 | Fat: 15g | Carbohydrates: 10g | Protein: 7g | Fiber: 5g | Sugars: 2g | Sodium: 150mg

Baked Eggplant Rounds with Low-Carb Marinara Sauce

Prep: 10 minutes | Cook: 25 minutes | Serves: 4

Ingredients:

- 1 large eggplant, sliced into rounds (550g)
- 1 cup low-carb marinara sauce (240g)
- 3/4 cup shredded mozzarella cheese (84g)
- 1/2 cup grated Parmesan cheese (50g)
- 3 tbsp olive oil (45ml)
- 1 tsp garlic powder (3g)
- Salt and pepper to taste
- Fresh basil for garnish

Instructions:

1. Preheat oven to 375°F (190°C).
2. Brush eggplant rounds with olive oil, sprinkle with garlic powder, salt, and pepper.
3. Place on a baking sheet and bake for 15 minutes.
4. Top each round with marinara sauce, mozzarella, and Parmesan cheese.
5. Bake for an additional 10 minutes or until cheese is melted and bubbly.
6. Garnish with fresh basil before serving.

Nutrition Facts (Per Serving): Calories: 220 | Fat: 16g | Carbohydrates: 12g | Protein: 12g | Fiber: 5g | Sugars: 6g | Sodium: 320mg

Garlic and Herb Baked Ricotta

Prep: 10 minutes | Cook: 15 minutes | Serves: 6

Ingredients:

- 1 1/2 cups ricotta cheese (375g)
- 3 cloves garlic, minced (9g)
- 3 tbsp chopped fresh herbs (basil, oregano) (45g)
- 2 eggs, beaten (100g)
- Salt and pepper to taste
- Olive oil for greasing
- 1/4 cup grated Parmesan cheese (25g)

Instructions:

1. Preheat the oven to 375°F (190°C).
2. In a mixing bowl, combine the ricotta, garlic, herbs, beaten eggs, Parmesan cheese, salt, and pepper. Mix well to ensure all ingredients are evenly distributed.
3. Grease a baking dish with olive oil to prevent sticking.
4. Pour the ricotta mixture into the dish, spreading it out evenly.
5. Place the dish in the oven and bake for about 15 minutes, or until the mixture is set and the top is golden brown.
6. Remove from the oven and allow to cool slightly before serving.

Nutrition Facts (Per Serving): Calories: 220 | Fat: 16g | Carbohydrates: 6g | Protein: 15g | Fiber: 0g | Sugars: 3g | Sodium: 200mg

Stuffed Tomatoes with Herbed Cream Cheese

Prep: 20 minutes | No Cook | Serves: 4

Ingredients:

- 4 large tomatoes (600g total)
- 1 cup cream cheese, light (240g)
- 1/4 cup chopped fresh herbs (parsley, chives) (60g)
- 1/2 tsp garlic powder (2g)
- Salt and pepper to taste
- 2 tbsp olive oil (30ml)
- 2 tbsp pine nuts (14g)

Instructions:

1. Slice the tops off the tomatoes and scoop out the insides.
2. In a mixing bowl, combine the light cream cheese, chopped herbs, garlic powder, salt, and pepper. Mix until smooth and well combined.
3. Drizzle a bit of olive oil inside each tomato before stuffing to add flavor and moisture.
4. Fill each tomato with the herbed cream cheese mixture, ensuring they are well stuffed.
5. Top each tomato with a sprinkle of pine nuts for an added texture.
6. Chill in the refrigerator for at least 30 minutes before serving.

Nutritional Facts (Per Serving): Calories: 220 | Fat: 18g | Carbohydrates: 10g | Protein: 6g | Fiber: 3g | Sugars: 6g | Sodium: 200mg

Creamy Spinach and Artichoke Dip

Prep: 10 minutes | Cook: 25 minutes | Serves: 4

Ingredients:

- 1 1/2 cups chopped frozen spinach, thawed and drained (270g)
- 1 1/2 cups canned artichoke hearts, drained and chopped (360g)
- 1/4 cup Greek yogurt (60ml) – for the base
- Salt and pepper to taste
- 1/4 cup light cream cheese (60g)
- 1/4 cup grated Parmesan cheese (25g)
- 2 tbsp Greek yogurt (30ml) – additional for consistency
- 3 cloves garlic, minced (9g)

Instructions:

1. Preheat the oven to 375°F (190°C).
2. In a mixing bowl, combine the spinach, artichoke hearts, Greek yogurt, light cream cheese, Parmesan cheese, minced garlic, salt, and pepper. Stir until the mixture is thoroughly blended.
3. Transfer the dip mixture into a baking dish, spreading it evenly.
4. Place the dish in the oven and bake for 20-25 minutes, or until the top is golden and the dip is bubbly. Allow the dip to cool slightly before serving.
5. Serve this dip with a side of low-carb vegetables or whole-grain crackers for a complete serving.

Nutritional Facts (Per Serving): Calories: 220 | Fat: 17g | Carbohydrates: 9g | Protein: 7g | Fiber: 3g | Sugars: 4g | Sodium: 320mg

Sundried Tomato and Basil Hummus with Whole Grain Crackers

Prep: 10 minutes | No Cook | Serves: 4

Ingredients:

- 2 cups chickpeas, cooked and drained (400g)
- 1/4 cup sundried tomatoes, chopped (30g)
- 2 tbsp tahini (30ml)
- Juice of 1 lemon (30ml)
- Salt and pepper to taste
- 1/4 cup fresh basil, chopped (15g)
- 2 cloves garlic, minced (6g)
- 2 tbsp olive oil (30ml)
- 2 Whole grain crackers per serving

Instructions:

1. In a food processor, blend the chickpeas, sundried tomatoes, tahini, lemon juice, basil, garlic, salt, pepper, and honey until the mixture reaches a smooth consistency.
2. If the hummus is too thick, add a little water or additional lemon juice to reach the desired consistency.
3. Taste and adjust the seasoning as needed.
4. Serve the hummus in a bowl, accompanied by whole grain crackers for dipping.

Nutrition Facts (Per Serving): Calories: 220 | Fat: 10g | Carbohydrates: 27g | Protein: 9g | Fiber: 6g | Sugars: 7g | Sodium: 220mg

Low-Carb Salsa Verde with Baked Chicken Thighs

Prep: 10 minutes | Cook: 25 minutes | Serves: 4

Ingredients:

- 4 medium chicken thighs, skinless (approx 120g each)
- 1 lb tomatillos, husked and rinsed (450g)
- 1/2 cup chopped white onion (70g)
- 1/4 cup chopped cilantro (15g)
- 2 cloves garlic, minced (6g)
- 1 jalapeño, seeded and chopped (14g)
- Juice of 1 lime (30ml)
- 1 tbsp olive oil (15ml) for chicken
- Salt and pepper to taste

Instructions:

1. Preheat your oven to 375°F (190°C).
Season the chicken thighs with salt and pepper, and brush with olive oil.
Place the chicken thighs on a baking sheet and bake for 25 minutes, or until the internal temperature reaches 165°F (74°C).
Combine tomatillos, onion, cilantro, garlic, jalapeño, and lime juice in a blender or food processor.
Pulse until the ingredients are finely chopped and mixed, but not pureed.
Season the salsa verde with salt, adjusting to taste.
Once the chicken is cooked, let serve topped with the fresh salsa verde.

Nutritional Facts (Per Serving): Calories: 220 | Fat: 10g | Carbohydrates: 27g | Protein: 9g | Fiber: 6g | Sugars: 7g | Sodium: 200mg

Zesty Lemon and Thyme Tapenade

Prep: 10 minutes | No Cook | Serves: 4

Ingredients:

- 3/4 cup pitted green olives (112.5g)
- Zest and juice of 1 lemon (30ml juice)
- 3 tbsp fresh thyme leaves (11.25g)
- 1 clove garlic, minced (3g)
- 1.5 tbsp capers, drained (22.5g)
- 3 tbsp olive oil (45ml)
- Salt and pepper to taste
- 8 whole grain crackers (2 crackers per serving)

Instructions:

1. In a food processor, combine olives, lemon zest, lemon juice, thyme, garlic, and capers. Pulse until coarsely chopped.
2. While processing, gradually add olive oil until the desired consistency is achieved.
3. Season with salt and pepper to taste.
4. Serve the tapenade evenly divided among four plates, accompanied by two whole grain crackers each.

Nutritional Facts (Per Serving): Calories: 220 | Fat: 20g | Carbohydrates: 8g | Protein: 1g | Fiber: 3g | Sugars: 2g | Sodium: 600mg

CHAPTER 10: DESSERTS AND BAKED GOODS
Guilt-Free Sweet Treats

Orange and Almond Flour Cake

Prep: 20 minutes | Cook: 30 minutes | Serves: 12

Ingredients:

- 3 cups almond flour (336g)
- 4 large eggs
- 1 cup sugar-free sweetener (erythritol) (240g)
- 1/2 cup fresh orange juice (120ml)
- Zest of 1 orange
- 1 tsp baking powder (5g)
- 1/4 tsp salt (1.25g)
- 1 tsp vanilla extract (5ml)

Instructions:

1. Preheat oven to 350°F (175°C). Grease a 9-inch round cake pan.
2. Beat eggs with sweetener until fluffy. Add orange juice, zest, and vanilla extract.
3. Stir in almond flour, baking powder, and salt.
4. Pour into the prepared pan and bake for 30 minutes or until a toothpick comes out clean. Cool before serving.

Nutritional Facts (Per Serving): Calories: 220 | Fat: 18g | Carbohydrates: 10g | Protein: 7g | Fiber: 3g | Sugars: 7g | Sodium: 100mg

No-Bake Peanut Butter Balls

Prep: 15 minutes | Cook: 0 minutes | Serves: 10

Ingredients:

- 1 cup natural peanut butter (250g)
- 1/4 cup honey (60ml)
- 3/4 cup almond flour (84g)
- 1/4 cup ground flaxseed (30g)
- 1/2 tsp vanilla extract (2.5ml)

Instructions:

1. In a large bowl, mix all ingredients until well combined.
2. Roll the mixture into small balls, about 1 inch in diameter.
3. Place on a baking sheet lined with parchment paper and refrigerate until firm, about 1 hour.

Nutrition Facts (Per Serving): Calories: 220 | Fat: 16g | Carbohydrates: 12g | Protein: 7g | Fiber: 3g | Sugars: 7g | Sodium: 0mg

Keto-Friendly Cheesecake with Almond Crust

Prep: 20 minutes | Cook: 50 minutes | Serves: 8

Ingredients:

- 2 cups almond flour (192g)
- 1/4 cup unsalted butter, melted (56g)
- 1 tbsp honey for crust (21g); 3 tbsp honey for filling (63g)
- 1 tbsp lemon juice (15ml)
- 1/4 tsp salt
- 24 oz cream cheese, softened (678g)
- 3 large eggs
- 1 tsp vanilla extract (5ml)

Instructions:

1. Preheat oven to 325°F (165°C). Mix almond flour, melted butter, and 1 tbsp of honey. Press into the bottom of a 9-inch springform pan. Bake for 10 minutes. Cool.
2. Beat cream cheese, 3 tbsp of honey, vanilla extract, and lemon juice until smooth. Add eggs one at a time. Pour over the crust.
3. Bake for 40 minutes or until set. Cool then refrigerate for 4 hours.

Nutritional Facts (Per Serving): Calories: 220 | Fat: 18g | Carbohydrates: 10g | Protein: 7g | Fiber: 2g | Sugars: 5g | Sodium: 220mg

Almond Flour Chocolate Chip Cookies

Prep: 10 minutes | Cook: 12 minutes | Serves: 10

Ingredients:

- 1 1/4 cups almond flour (140g)
- 1/4 cup butter, softened (56g)
- 1/4 cup honey (60ml)
- 1/2 tsp vanilla extract (2.5ml)
- 1/2 large egg
- 1/4 tsp baking soda (1.25g)
- A pinch of salt
- 1/4 cup sugar-free chocolate chips (42.5g)

Instructions:

1. Preheat oven to 350°F (175°C).
2. In a mixing bowl, cream together the butter and honey until smooth. Add the vanilla and egg, and continue mixing until well combined.
2. Combine almond flour, baking soda, and salt. Add to the butter mixture and mix until combined.
3. Stir in chocolate chips.
4. Drop dough by tablespoonfuls onto a baking sheet. Flatten slightly.
5. Bake for 12 minutes or until edges are golden.
6. Cool on the baking sheet for 5 minutes before transferring to a wire rack.

Nutritional Facts (Per Serving 1 Cookies): Calories: 220 | Fat: 20g | Carbohydrates: 8g | Protein: 1g | Fiber: 3g | Sugars: 2g | Sodium: 600mg

Raspberry Almond Flour Scones

Prep: 15 minutes | Cook: 20 minutes | Serves: 8

Ingredients:

- 2 cups almond flour (224g)
- 1/3 cup coconut flour (40g)
- 1/4 cup honey (60ml)
- 1 tsp baking powder (4g)
- 1/4 tsp salt (1.5g)
- 1/4 cup unsalted butter, cold and cubed (60g)
- 2 large eggs
- 1/2 tsp almond extract (2.5ml)
- 1 cup raspberries (123g)

Instructions:

1. Preheat oven to 350°F (175°C). Line a baking sheet with parchment paper.
2. In a large bowl, mix almond flour, coconut flour, baking powder, and salt.
3. Cut in butter until the mixture resembles coarse crumbs.
4. In a separate bowl, whisk together eggs, honey, and almond extract. Add to the dry ingredients, stirring until just combined.
5. Gently fold in raspberries.
6. Form dough into a circle on the prepared baking sheet, then cut into 8 wedges.
7. Bake for 25 minutes or until golden brown. Let cool before serving.

Nutrition Facts (Per Serving): Calories: 220 | Fat: 18g | Carbohydrates: 14g | Protein: 6g | Fiber: 4g | Sugars: 7g | Sodium: 100mg

Sugar-Free Lemon Bars

Prep: 15 minutes | Cook: 45 minutes | Serves: 8

Ingredients:

- 1 cup almond flour (112g)
- 1/4 cup coconut oil, melted (60ml)
- 2 tbsp honey (30ml)

For the filling:
- 3 large eggs
- 1/2 cup honey (120ml)
- 1/2 cup lemon juice (120ml)
- 2 tbsp lemon zest (10g)
- 2 tbsp coconut flour (16g)

Instructions:

1. Preheat oven to 350°F (175°C). Line an 8x8 inch baking pan with parchment paper.
2. Combine almond flour, coconut oil, and honey for the crust. Press into the bottom of the prepared pan.
3. Bake crust for 10 minutes.
For the filling, whisk together eggs, honey, lemon juice, lemon zest, and coconut flour until smooth.
4. Pour filling over the pre-baked crust. Return to oven and bake for an additional 20 minutes.
5. Cool completely before cutting into bars.

Nutrition Facts (Per Serving): Calories: 220 | Fat: 15g | Carbohydrates: 17g | Protein: 5g | Fiber: 2g | Sugars: 12g | Sodium: 70mg

Coconut and Chia Seed Pudding

Prep: 10 minutes | Cook: 0 minutes | Serves: 4

Ingredients:

- 1 can coconut milk (400ml)
- 1/4 cup chia seeds (40g)
- 2 tbsp honey (30ml)
- 1/2 tsp vanilla extract (2.5ml)
- 1/4 cup raspberries for topping (31g)
- 1 tbsp shredded coconut for topping (5g)

Instructions:

1. In a bowl, mix coconut milk, chia seeds, honey, and vanilla extract until well combined.
2. Divide the mixture into serving dishes and refrigerate overnight or at least 6 hours until set.
3. Top with raspberries and shredded coconut before serving.

Nutrition Facts (Per Serving): Calories: 220 | Fat: 18g | Carbohydrates: 12g | Protein: 3g | Fiber: 5g | Sugars: 6g | Sodium: 15mg

Sugar-Free Lemon Ricotta Cheesecake

Prep: 15 minutes | Cook: 35 minutes | Serves: 4

Ingredients:

- 1 1/2 cups almond flour (150g)
- 3/4 cup ricotta cheese (180g)
- 2 tsp sugar-free sweetener
- 4 eggs
- 1 lemon, zested and juiced (zest: 5g, juice: 45ml)
- 1 tsp baking powder (4g)
- 1 tsp vanilla extract (5ml)

Instructions:

1. Preheat oven to 350°F (175°C). Grease an 8-inch cake pan and line with parchment paper.
2. In a large bowl, mix together ricotta, sugar-free sweetener, lemon zest, lemon juice, and vanilla extract.
3. Beat in eggs one at a time. Gently fold in almond flour and baking powder until well combined.
4. Pour batter into the prepared pan and bake for 35 minutes, or until a toothpick comes out clean. Let cool before serving.

Nutrition Facts (Per Serving): Calories: 220 | Fat: 15g | Carbohydrates: 13g | Protein: 9g | Fiber: 2g | Sugars: 4g | Sodium: 150mg

CHAPTER 11: DESSERTS AND BAKED GOODS
Baked Goods and Pastries

Low-Carb Lemon Ricotta Cake

Prep: 10 minutes | Cook: 35 minutes | Serves: 8

Ingredients:

- 1 1/2 cups almond flour (150g)
- 3/4 cup ricotta cheese (180g)
- 1/4 cup honey (60ml)
- 4 eggs
- 1 lemon, zested and juiced (zest: 5g, juice: 45ml)
- 1 tsp baking powder (4g)
- 1 tsp vanilla extract (5ml)

Instructions:

1. Preheat oven to 350°F (175°C). Grease an 8-inch cake pan and line with parchment paper.
2. In a large bowl, mix together ricotta, honey, lemon zest, lemon juice, and vanilla extract.
3. Beat in eggs one at a time. Gently fold in almond flour and baking powder until well combined.
4. Pour batter into prepared pan and bake for 35 minutes, or until a toothpick comes out clean.
5. Let cool before serving.

Nutrition Facts (Per Serving): Calories: 220 | Fat: 15g | Carbohydrates: 13g | Protein: 9g | Fiber: 2g | Sugars: 9g | Sodium: 150mg

Coconut and Raspberry Friands

Prep: 15 minutes | Cook: 20 minutes | Serves:12

Ingredients:

- 1 cup almond flour (100g)
- 1/2 cup desiccated coconut (40g)
- 1/4 cup honey (60ml)
- 4 egg whites
- 1/2 cup melted coconut oil (120ml)
- 1/2 cup raspberries (61g)

Instructions:

1. Preheat oven to 350°F (175°C). Grease a 12-cup friand or muffin tin.
2. In a bowl, mix almond flour, desiccated coconut, and honey.
3. Stir in egg whites and melted coconut oil until well combined.
4. Divide mixture among prepared cups, pressing a few raspberries into each.
5. Bake for 25 minutes, or until golden and a toothpick comes out clean. Let cool before serving.

Nutrition Facts (Per Serving): Calories: 220 | Fat: 18g | Carbohydrates: 10g | Protein: 4g | Fiber: 3g | Sugars: 7g | Sodium: 45mg

Sugar-Free Cranberry and Orange Loaf

Prep: 15 minutes | Cook: 50 minutes | Serves:10

Ingredients:

- 2 cups almond flour (224g)
- 1 tsp baking powder (4g)
- 1/4 tsp salt (1.5g)
- 1/2 cup unsweetened cranberries, chopped (50g)
- Zest of 1 orange (2 tbsp, 6g)
- 1/4 cup coconut oil, melted (60ml)
- 1/4 cup honey (60ml)
- 3 eggs
- 1/2 tsp vanilla extract (2.5ml)
- Juice of 1 orange (1/4 cup, 60ml)

Instructions:

1. Preheat oven to 350°F (175°C). Grease a loaf pan and line with parchment paper.
2. In a large bowl, mix almond flour, baking powder, salt, cranberries, and orange zest.
3. In another bowl, whisk together coconut oil, honey, eggs, vanilla extract, and orange juice.
4. Combine wet and dry ingredients and stir until just mixed.
5. Pour batter into prepared loaf pan. Bake for 50 minutes, or until a toothpick inserted into the center comes out clean.

Nutrition Facts (Per Serving): Calories: 220 | Fat: 18g | Carbohydrates: 12g | Protein: 6g | Fiber: 3g | Sugars: 7g | Sodium: 150mg

Almond and Orange Zest Biscotti

Prep: 15 minutes | Cook: 45 minutes | Serves:10

Ingredients:

- 2 cups almond flour (192g)
- 1/4 cup honey (60ml)
- 1 tsp baking powder (4g)
- 1/4 tsp salt (1.5g)
- 3 large eggs
- 1 tsp vanilla extract (5ml)
- 1/2 tsp almond extract (2.5ml)
- Orange zest (from 1 orange or 6g)
- 1/2 cup whole almonds, roughly chopped (70g)

Instructions:

1. Preheat oven to 350°F (175°C). Line a baking sheet with parchment paper.
2. In a large bowl, combine almond flour, honey, baking powder, and salt.
3. Beat in eggs, vanilla extract, almond extract, and orange zest until well mixed.
4. Fold in chopped almonds.
5. Form the dough into a log shape on the prepared baking sheet. Bake for 25 minutes.
6. Remove from oven, let cool for 15 minutes, then slice diagonally into 1/2-inch thick slices.
7. Place slices back on the baking sheet and bake for an additional 20 minutes, turning halfway through, until crisp.

Nutritional Facts (Per Serving): Calories: 210 | Sugars: 1g | Fat: 16g | Carbohydrates: 8g | Protein: 7g | Fiber: 3g | Sodium: 75m

CHAPTER 12: DESSERTS AND BAKED GOODS
Frozen Desserts and Puddings

Keto Lemon and Blueberry Frozen Yogurt

Prep: 10 minutes | **Cook:** 0 minutes | **Freeze:** 2 hours | **Serves:** 4

Ingredients:

- 2 cups Greek yogurt (full-fat, 480g)
- 2 tbsp keto-friendly sweetener (30g)
- 1 tbsp lemon zest (6g)
- 1/4 cup lemon juice (60ml)
- 1/2 cup blueberries (75g)

Instructions:

1. Blend Greek yogurt, keto-friendly sweetener, lemon juice, lemon zest, and vanilla extract until smooth.
2. Fold in blueberries.
3. Pour mixture into a freezer-safe container and freeze for 2 hours, stirring every 30 minutes for a smoother texture.
4. Serve frozen.

Nutritional Facts (Per Serving): Calories: 210 | Sugars: 3g | Fat: 15g | Carbohydrates: 8g | Protein: 10g | Fiber: 1g | Sodium: 45mg

Mixed Berry Coconut Milk Sherbet

Prep: 10 minutes | **Cook:** 0 minutes | **Freeze:** 2 hours | **Serves:** 6

Ingredients:

- 2 cups mixed berries, fresh or frozen (300g)
- 1 can coconut milk (400ml)
- 1/4 cup low-calorie sweetener (48g)
- 1 tsp lemon juice (5ml)

Instructions:

1. In a blender, combine mixed berries, coconut milk, your chosen sweetener, and lemon juice. Blend until smooth.
2. Pour mixture into a freezer-safe container and freeze for about 4 hours, stirring every hour to help break up ice crystals.
3. Serve frozen.

Nutrition Facts (Per Serving): Calories: 200 | Fat: 14g | Carbohydrates: 8g | Protein: 2g | Fiber: 2g | Sugars: 3g | Sodium: 20mg

Almond Milk and Vanilla Bean Panna Cotta

Prep: 15 minutes | Cook: 5 minutes | Chill: 4 hours | Serves: 4

Ingredients:

- 2 cups almond milk (480ml)
- 1 vanilla bean, split and seeds scraped (or 1 tsp vanilla extract) (5ml)
- 1/4 cup keto-friendly sweetener (48g)
- 2 tsp gelatin powder (10g)
- 2 tbsp water (30ml)

Instructions:

1. Sprinkle gelatin over water in a small bowl and let stand for 5 minutes to soften.
2. In a saucepan, heat almond milk and vanilla bean seeds (or extract) just to a simmer. Do not boil.
3. Remove from heat and add softened gelatin, stirring until completely dissolved.
4. Stir in your chosen keto-friendly sweetener until dissolved.
5. Pour into 4 serving glasses and refrigerate for at least 4 hours, or until set.

Nutrition Facts (Per Serving): Calories: 50 | Fat: 3g | Carbohydrates: 1g | Protein: 2g | Fiber: 0g | Sugars: 0g | Sodium: 80mg

Sugar-Free Mint Chocolate Chip Ice Cream

Prep: 10 minutes | Cook: 0 minutes | Freeze: 4 hours | Serves: 8

Ingredients:

- 2 cups heavy cream (480ml)
- 1 cup unsweetened almond milk (240ml)
- 3/4 cup low-calorie sweetener (150g)
- A pinch of salt (0.5g)
- 1/2 cup fresh mint leaves, finely chopped (120g)
- 1 tsp vanilla extract (5ml)
- 1/2 cup sugar-free dark chocolate, chopped (85g)

Instructions:

1. In a large bowl, whisk together heavy cream, almond milk, sweetener, chopped mint leaves, vanilla extract, pinch of salt until sweetener is dissolved.
2. Pour the mixture into an ice cream maker and churn according to the manufacturer's instructions, until it reaches a soft-serve consistency.
3. Just before the ice cream is done, add the chopped sugar-free dark chocolate and allow it to mix thoroughly.
4. Transfer the ice cream to a freezer-safe container and freeze for at least 4 hours.

Nutritional Facts (Per Serving): Calories: 210 | Sugars: 2g | Fat: 20g | Carbohydrates: 9g | Protein: 2g | Fiber: 1g | Sodium: 25mg

CHAPTER 13: DINNER
Simple Weeknight Dinners

Mediterranean-Style Baked Cod with Tomatoes and Olives

Prep: 15 minutes | Cook: 25 minutes | Serves: 4

Ingredients:

- Cod fillets (4 pieces, 6oz or 170g each)
- Olive oil (2 tbsp or 30ml)
- Cherry tomatoes (1 cup or 150g), halved
- Black olives (1/4 cup or 30g), pitted and sliced
- Garlic cloves (2 or 6g), minced
- Lemon juice (1 tbsp or 15ml)
- Fresh basil (2 tbsp or 8g), chopped
- Salt and pepper to taste

Instructions:

1. Preheat oven to 400°F (200°C). In a baking dish, place cod fillets and season with salt and pepper.
2. Scatter cherry tomatoes, olives, and garlic around the cod. Drizzle with olive oil and lemon juice.
3. Bake for 20-25 minutes or until cod is flaky and cooked through.
4. Garnish with fresh basil before serving.

Nutritional Facts (Per Serving): Calories: 360 | Sugars: 3g | Fat: 14g | Carbohydrates: 8g | Protein: 50g | Fiber: 2g | Sodium: 300mg

Grilled Salmon with Avocado Salsa

Prep: 15 minutes | Cook: 10 minutes | Serves: 4

Ingredients:

- 4 pieces salmon fillets (6 oz or 170g each)
- 1 tbsp olive oil (15ml)
- Salt and pepper to taste
- 1 large avocado, diced (200g)
- 1 medium tomato, diced (100g)
- 1/4 cup red onion, finely chopped (40g)
- 2 tbsp lime juice (30ml)
- 2 tbsp fresh cilantro, chopped (8g)

Instructions:

1. Preheat grill to medium-high heat.
2. Brush salmon with olive oil, season with salt and pepper.
3. Grill salmon for 5 minutes per side or until desired doneness.
4. Mix avocado, tomato, onion, lime juice, and cilantro in a bowl. Season with salt and pepper.
5. Serve salmon topped with avocado salsa.

Nutritional Facts (Per Serving): Calories: 380 | Sugars: 2g | Fat: 22g | Carbohydrates: 9g | Protein: 34g | Fiber: 5g | Sodium: 200mg

Lemon Herb Cod with Cauliflower Mash

Prep: 15 minutes | **Cook:** 20 minutes | **Serves:** 4

Ingredients:

- 4 cod fillets (4 oz or 113g each)
- 1 head cauliflower, cut into florets (600g)
- 2 tbsp olive oil (30ml)
- 1 lemon, juiced and zested (50ml juice, 5g zest)
- 2 garlic cloves, minced (6g)
- 2 tbsp fresh parsley, chopped (8g)
- Salt and pepper to taste

Instructions:

1. Preheat oven to 375°F (190°C). Line a baking tray with parchment paper.
2. Place cod fillets on tray. Drizzle with 1 tbsp olive oil, lemon juice, and season with salt, pepper, and half the lemon zest. Bake for 15-20 minutes.
3. Meanwhile, steam cauliflower until very tender, about 10 minutes. Blend steamed cauliflower with remaining olive oil, garlic, and parsley until smooth.
4. Season with salt and pepper.
5. Serve cod over cauliflower mash, garnished with remaining lemon zest.

Nutritional Facts (Per Serving): Calories: 380 | Fat: 14g | Carbohydrates: 15g | Protein: 45g | Fiber: 5g | Sugars: 5g | Sodium: 150mg

Garlic Shrimp Zoodles with Pesto

Prep: 15 minutes | **Cook:** 10 minutes | **Serves:** 4

Ingredients:

- 1 lb (450g) shrimp, peeled and deveined
- 4 medium zucchinis, spiralized (400g)
- 2 tbsp olive oil (30ml)
- 3 garlic cloves, minced (9g)
- 1/4 cup basil pesto (60ml)
- Salt and pepper to taste
- Fresh basil leaves for garnish (5g)

Instructions:

1. Heat 1 tbsp olive oil in a large pan over medium heat. Add garlic and shrimp, season with salt and pepper, and cook until shrimp are pink and cooked through, about 4-5 minutes. Remove shrimp from the pan.
2. In the same pan, add remaining olive oil and zoodles. Sauté for 2-3 minutes until just tender.
3. Return shrimp to the pan with zoodles. Add pesto and toss to combine. Heat through for 1-2 minutes.
4. Serve garnished with fresh basil leaves.

Nutritional Facts (Per Serving): Calories: 380 | Fat: 18g | Carbohydrates: 10g | Protein: 40g | Fiber: 2g | Sugars: 4g | Sodium: 300mg

Seafood Paella with Brown Rice

Prep: 20 minutes | Cook: 40 minutes | Serves: 4

Ingredients:

- 1 cup brown rice (190g)
- 4 cups chicken broth (960ml)
- 2 tbsp olive oil (30ml)
- 1 medium onion, finely chopped (110g)
- 1 bell pepper, diced (150g)
- 2 garlic cloves, minced (6g)
- Lemon wedges for serving
- 1 tsp paprika (2g)
- 1 large tomato, diced (180g)
- A pinch saffron threads (0.1g)
- Salt and pepper to taste
- 1 lb mixed seafood (shrimp, mussels, and calamari, 450g total)
- 1/2 cup peas (65g)

Instructions:

1. In a large skillet, heat olive oil over medium heat. Add onion, bell pepper, and garlic, sauté until soft.
2. Stir in tomato, paprika, saffron, salt, and pepper. Add brown rice and chicken broth, bring to a boil.
3. Reduce heat to low, cover, and simmer for 30 minutes.
4. Add seafood and peas, cover, and cook for an additional 10 minutes or until seafood is cooked through and rice is tender.
5. Serve hot with lemon wedges.

Nutritional Facts (Per Serving): Calories: 380 | Sugars: 3g | Fat: 10g | Carbohydrates: 45g | Protein: 25g | Fiber: 4g | Sodium: 700mg

Spicy Tuna Stuffed Avocados

Prep: 15 minutes | Cook: 0 minutes | Serves: 4

Ingredients:

- 2 avocados, halved and pitted (200g each)
- 1 can tuna in water, drained (120g)
- 2 tbsp mayonnaise (30ml)
- 1 tbsp Sriracha sauce, or to taste (15ml)
- 1 tbsp lime juice (15ml)
- 1/4 cup diced red onion (40g)
- Salt and pepper to taste
- Fresh cilantro for garnish (optional, 4g)

Instructions:

1. In a bowl, mix the tuna, mayonnaise, Sriracha sauce, lime juice, and diced red onion. Season with salt and pepper.
2. Scoop out some of the avocado flesh to make room for the tuna mixture. Chop the scooped avocado and stir it into the tuna mixture.
3. Fill avocado halves with the spicy tuna mixture. Garnish with fresh cilantro if desired.
4. Serve immediately or chill until serving.

Nutritional Facts (Per Serving): Calories: 380 | Fat: 25g | Carbohydrates: 12g | Protein: 25g | Fiber: 7g | Sugars: 2g | Sodium: 320mg

CHAPTER 14: DINNER
Vegetable Evening Feasts

Grilled Zucchini and Bell Pepper with Feta

Prep: 15 minutes | Cook: 30 minutes | Serves: 4

Ingredients:

- 2 zucchinis, sliced lengthwise (400g)
- 2 bell peppers, sliced (300g)
- 2 tbsp olive oil (30ml)
- Salt and pepper to taste
- 1/2 cup feta cheese, crumbled (75g)
- Fresh basil, chopped (2 tbsp or 8g) for garnish

Instructions:

1. Preheat grill to medium-high heat. Brush zucchini and bell pepper slices with olive oil and season with salt and pepper.
2. Grill vegetables for about 3-5 minutes per side, until charred and tender.
3. Arrange grilled vegetables on a platter, sprinkle with crumbled feta cheese, and garnish with chopped basil.

Nutritional Facts (Per Serving): Calories: 380 | Fat: 25g | Carbohydrates: 30g | Protein: 10g | Fiber: 5g | Sugars: 8g | Sodium: 400mg

Cucumber and Yogurt Salad with Dill

Prep: 10 minutes | Cook: 0 minutes | Serves: 4

Ingredients:

- 2 large cucumbers, diced (500g)
- 1 cup Greek yogurt (245g)
- 2 tbsp fresh dill, chopped (8g)
- 1 garlic clove, minced (3g)
- 2 tbsp lemon juice (30ml)
- Salt and pepper to taste

Instructions:

1. In a large bowl, combine diced cucumbers, Greek yogurt, chopped dill, minced garlic, and lemon juice. Stir until well mixed.
2. Season with salt and pepper to taste.
3. Chill in the refrigerator for at least 30 minutes before serving to allow flavors to meld.
4. Serve cold, garnished with additional dill if desired.

Nutritional Facts (Per Serving): Calories: 380 | Fat: 10g | Carbohydrates: 12g | Protein: 8g | Fiber: 2g | Sugars: 6g | Sodium: 100mg

Quinoa Salad with Roasted Vegetables

Prep: 20 minutes | Cook: 30 minutes | Serves: 4

Ingredients:

- 1 cup quinoa (170g), rinsed
- 2 cups water (480ml)
- 1 medium zucchini, cubed (200g)
- 1 red bell pepper, cubed (150g)
- 1 yellow bell pepper, cubed (150g)
- 1 small red onion, chopped (100g)
- 2 tbsp olive oil (30ml)
- 2 tbsp balsamic vinegar (30ml)
- 1 tbsp honey (15ml)
- Salt and pepper to taste
- 1/4 cup fresh basil, chopped (10g)

Instructions:

1. Preheat oven to 425°F (220°C). Toss zucchini, bell peppers, and red onion with 1 tbsp olive oil, salt, and pepper. Spread on a baking sheet and roast for 20 minutes.
2. Meanwhile, bring water to a boil in a medium pot. Add quinoa, reduce heat to low, cover, and simmer for 15 minutes. Fluff with a fork and let cool.
3. Whisk together remaining olive oil, balsamic vinegar, and honey for the dressing.
4. In a large bowl, mix roasted vegetables, quinoa, and dressing. Adjust seasoning if needed.

Nutritional Facts (Per Serving): Calories: 380 | Fat: 10g | Carbohydrates: 60g | Protein: 10g | Fiber: 8g | Sugars: 10g | Sodium: 200mg

Eggplant and Zucchini Lasagna

Prep: 30 minutes | Cook: 45 minutes | Serves: 4

Ingredients:

- 1 large eggplant, sliced (500g)
- 2 large zucchinis, sliced (400g)
- 1 cup cashews, soaked for 4 hours (150g)
- 1/2 cup water (120ml)
- 1 lemon, juiced (2 tbsp or 30ml)
- 2 tbsp nutritional yeast (8g)
- 1 clove garlic, minced (3g)
- Salt and pepper to taste
- 2 cups marinara sauce (480ml)
- 1 tbsp olive oil (15ml)
- Fresh basil for garnish (5g)

Instructions:

1. Preheat oven to 375°F (190°C). Brush eggplant and zucchini slices with olive oil and season with salt and pepper. Grill or broil slices until tender, about 5 minutes per side.
2. Blend cashews, water, lemon juice, nutritional yeast, garlic, salt, and pepper until smooth to make the cashew cheese.
3. Layer grilled eggplant, zucchini, cashew cheese, and marinara sauce in a baking dish. Repeat layers.
4. Cover with foil and bake for 30 minutes. Uncover and bake for another 15 minutes until bubbly.
5. Garnish with fresh basil before serving.

Nutritional Facts (Per Serving): Calories: 380 | Fat: 22g | Carbohydrates: 35g | Protein: 15g | Fiber: 9g | Sugars: 13g | Sodium: 600mg

Spinach and Feta Stuffed Portobello Mushrooms

Prep: 15 minutes | Cook: 20 minutes | Serves: 4

Ingredients:

- 4 large Portobello mushrooms, stems removed (300g)
- 2 cups spinach, chopped (60g)
- 1/2 cup feta cheese, crumbled (75g)
- 1/4 cup Greek yogurt (60ml)
- 2 cloves garlic, minced (6g)
- 2 tbsp olive oil (30ml)
- Salt and pepper to taste
- Fresh thyme for garnish (2g)

Instructions:

1. Preheat oven to 375°F (190°C). Brush mushrooms with 1 tbsp olive oil and season with salt and pepper. Place on a baking sheet, gill-side up.
2. In a bowl, mix spinach, feta cheese, Greek yogurt, garlic, and remaining olive oil. Season with salt and pepper.
3. Stuff each mushroom cap with the spinach mixture. Bake for 20 minutes, or until mushrooms are tender and filling is golden.
4. Garnish with fresh thyme before serving.

Nutritional Facts (Per Serving): Calories: 380 | Fat: 25g | Carbohydrates: 20g | Protein: 15g | Fiber: 5g | Sugars: 8g | Sodium: 500mg

Broccoli and Couscous Salad with Honey Mustard Dressing

Prep: 15 minutes | Cook: 10 minutes | Serves: 4

Ingredients:

- 1 cup couscous (200g), uncooked
- 1 1/4 cups water (300ml)
- 4 cups broccoli florets (300g)
- 2 tbsp olive oil (30ml) for dressing
- 2 tbsp honey (30ml) for dressing
- 2 tbsp Dijon mustard (30ml) for dressing
- 1 lemon, juiced (2 tbsp or 30ml) for dressing
- Salt and pepper to taste
- 1/4 cup sliced almonds (30g) for garnish

Instructions:

1. In a medium saucepan, bring water to a boil. Add couscous, remove from heat, cover, and let stand until water is absorbed, about 5 minutes. Fluff with a fork and let cool.
2. Steam broccoli florets until just tender, about 3-4 minutes. Let cool.
3. For the dressing, whisk together olive oil, honey, Dijon mustard, and lemon juice in a small bowl. Season with salt and pepper.
4. In a large bowl, combine cooled couscous, broccoli, and dressing. Toss until well mixed.
5. Garnish with sliced almonds before serving.

Nutritional Facts (Per Serving): Calories: 380 | Fat: 14g | Carbohydrates: 55g | Protein: 12g | Fiber: 5g | Sugars: 10g | Sodium: 200mg

CHAPTER 15: DINNER
Sea Special Occasion Dishes

Chilean Sea Bass with Pomegranate Salsa and Couscous

Prep: 20 minutes | Cook: 15 minutes | Serves: 4

Ingredients:

- 4 pieces Chilean sea bass (6 oz or 170g each)
- 1 cup couscous (180g), cooked
- 1/2 cup pomegranate seeds (88g)
- 1/4 cup red onion, finely chopped (40g)
- 1/4 cup cilantro, chopped (4g)
- 2 tbsp olive oil (30ml), plus more for brushing
- 1 tbsp lemon juice (15ml)
- Salt and pepper to taste

Instructions:

1. Preheat the oven to 400°F (200°C). Brush sea bass with olive oil, season with salt and pepper. Bake for 12-15 minutes, until flaky.
2. Mix pomegranate seeds, red onion, cilantro, olive oil, and lemon juice for salsa. Season with salt.
3. Serve sea bass over cooked couscous, topped with pomegranate salsa.

Nutritional Facts (Per Serving): Calories: 380 | Fat: 10g | Carbohydrates: 35g | Protein: 35g | Fiber: 3g | Sugars: 5g | Sodium: 200mg

Oyster Mushroom and Spinach Stuffed Salmon

Prep: 25 minutes | Cook: 20 minutes | Serves: 4

Ingredients:

- 4 pieces salmon fillets (6 oz or 170g each), pocketed for stuffing
- 2 cups spinach, sautéed (60g)
- 1 cup oyster mushrooms, chopped and sautéed (70g)
- 2 tbsp Greek yogurt (30ml)
- 1 garlic clove, minced (3g)
- 2 tbsp fresh dill, chopped (8g)
- Salt and pepper to taste
- 1 tbsp olive oil (15ml) for brushing

Instructions:

1. Preheat oven to 375°F (190°C). Mix sautéed spinach, mushrooms, Greek yogurt, garlic, and dill.
2. Season with salt and pepper.
3. Stuff salmon pockets with the mixture. Brush with olive oil, season.
4. Bake for 18-20 minutes. Serve immediately.

Nutritional Facts (Per Serving): Calories: 380 | Fat: 20g | Carbohydrates: 5g | Protein: 45g | Fiber: 2g | Sugars: 2g | Sodium: 300mg

Salmon en Papillote with Vegetables

Prep: 15 minutes | Cook: 20 minutes | Serves: 4

Ingredients:

- 4 pieces salmon fillets (6 oz or 170g each)
- 1 medium zucchini, thinly sliced (200g)
- 2 medium carrots, thinly sliced (150g)
- 1 bell pepper, thinly sliced (150g)
- 2 tbsp olive oil (30ml)
- 8 slices lemon
- 2 tbsp fresh dill (8g)
- Salt and pepper to taste

Instructions:

1. Preheat oven to 400°F (200°C). Cut 4 pieces of parchment paper large enough to wrap each salmon fillet and vegetables.
2. Divide the vegetables among the parchment papers, top with a salmon fillet, and season with salt and pepper. Place 2 lemon slices on each and sprinkle with dill. Drizzle with olive oil.
3. Fold the parchment paper over the salmon and vegetables, twisting the ends to seal.
4. Bake for 20 minutes. Serve immediately in the parchment for a steamy reveal.

Nutritional Facts (Per Serving): Calories: 380 | Sugars: 4g | Fat: 20g | Carbohydrates: 10g | Protein: 35g | Fiber: 3g | Sodium: 200mg

Grilled Swordfish with Mediterranean Salsa

Prep: 15 minutes | Cook: 10 minutes | Serves: 4

Ingredients:

- 4 pieces swordfish steaks (6 oz or 170g each)
- 2 tbsp olive oil (30ml)
- Salt and pepper to taste
- 1 cup cherry tomatoes, halved (150g)
- 1/2 cucumber, diced (100g)
- 1/4 cup red onion, finely chopped (40g)
- 1/4 cup Kalamata olives, chopped (50g)
- 1/4 cup feta cheese, crumbled (50g)
- 2 tbsp lemon juice (30ml)
- 2 tbsp fresh parsley, chopped (8g)

Instructions:

1. Preheat grill to medium-high heat. Brush swordfish steaks with olive oil and season with salt and pepper.
2. Grill swordfish for about 5 minutes per side, until cooked through.
3. Combine tomatoes, cucumber, red onion, olives, feta, lemon juice, and parsley in a bowl for the salsa. Season with salt and pepper.
4. Serve grilled swordfish topped with Mediterranean salsa.

Nutritional Facts (Per Serving): Calories: 350 | Sugars: 4g | Fat: 18g | Carbohydrates: 8g | Protein: 38g | Fiber: 2g | Sodium: 350mg

Tilapia with Fennel and Orange Salad

Prep: 15 minutes | Cook: 10 minutes | Serves: 4

Ingredients:

- 4 pieces tilapia fillets (6 oz or 170g each)
- 2 tbsp olive oil (30ml)
- 1 large fennel bulb, thinly sliced (200g)
- 2 oranges, segmented (300g)
- 1/4 cup red onion, thinly sliced (40g)
- 1 tbsp lemon juice (15ml)
- Salt and pepper to taste
- 2 tbsp fresh dill, chopped (8g)

Instructions:

1. Season tilapia with salt and pepper. Heat olive oil in a skillet over medium heat and cook tilapia for about 4-5 minutes per side, until golden and flaky.
2. Combine fennel, orange segments, red onion, lemon juice, and dill in a bowl. Season with salt and pepper.
3. Serve tilapia topped with fennel and orange salad.

Nutritional Facts (Per Serving): Calories: 360 | Sugars: 6g | Fat: 12g | Carbohydrates: 15g | Protein: 48g | Fiber: 3g | Sodium: 200mg

Herb-Crusted Haddock with Steamed Vegetables

Prep: 15 minutes | Cook: 20 minutes | Serves: 4

Ingredients:

- 4 pieces haddock fillets (6 oz or 170g each)
- 1/2 cup whole wheat breadcrumbs (60g)
- 2 tbsp fresh parsley, chopped (8g)
- 1 tsp fresh thyme, chopped (1g)
- 1 tbsp lemon zest (6g)
- 2 tbsp olive oil (30ml)
- 2 cups mixed vegetables (carrots, broccoli, cauliflower), for steaming (300g)
- Salt and pepper to taste

Instructions:

1. Preheat oven to 400°F (200°C). Mix breadcrumbs, parsley, thyme, lemon zest, salt, and pepper in a bowl.
2. Brush haddock fillets with olive oil and coat with the breadcrumb mixture.
3. Place on a baking sheet and bake for 15-20 minutes or until the crust is golden and fish flakes easily.
4. Steam mixed vegetables until tender, about 5-7 minutes.
5. Serve haddock with steamed vegetables on the side.

Nutritional Facts (Per Serving): Calories: 350 | Sugars: 3g | Fat: 12g | Carbohydrates: 20g | Protein: 40g | Fiber: 4g | Sodium: 200mg

Baked Stuffed Flounder with Spinach and Feta

Prep: 20 minutes | Cook: 25 minutes | Serves: 4

Ingredients:

- 4 pieces flounder fillets (6 oz or 170g each)
- 2 cups spinach, sautéed and squeezed dry (60g)
- 1/2 cup feta cheese, crumbled (75g)
- 1 garlic clove, minced (3g)
- 1 tbsp lemon juice (15ml)
- Olive oil (for brushing)
- Salt and pepper to taste

Instructions:

1. Preheat oven to 375°F (190°C). Mix spinach, feta, garlic, and lemon juice in a bowl.
2. Lay flounder fillets flat and divide the spinach mixture among them. Roll up each fillet and secure with a toothpick.
3. Place the stuffed fillets in a greased baking dish. Brush with olive oil and season with salt and pepper.
4. Bake for 20-25 minutes or until fish is cooked through. Serve hot.

Nutritional Facts (Per Serving): Calories: 370 | Sugars: 2g | Fat: 16g | Carbohydrates: 5g | Protein: 50g | Fiber: 1g | Sodium: 400mg

Miso Glazed Halibut with Bok Choy Stir-Fry

Prep: 15 minutes | Cook: 20 minutes | Serves: 4

Ingredients:

- 4 pieces halibut fillets (6 oz or 170g each)
- 2 tbsp miso paste (30ml)
- 1 tbsp honey (15ml)
- 1 tbsp olive oil (15ml), plus extra for brushing
- Salt and pepper to taste
- 4 cups bok choy, chopped (360g)
- 2 garlic cloves, minced (6g)
- 1 tbsp soy sauce (low sodium) (15ml)
- 1 tsp ginger, grated (2g)

Instructions:

1. Preheat oven to 400°F (200°C). Mix miso paste, honey, and 1 tbsp olive oil for the glaze. Brush halibut with this glaze.
2. Place halibut on a baking sheet lined with parchment. Bake for 12-15 minutes, until cooked through.
3. Heat a bit of olive oil in a skillet over medium heat. Sauté garlic and ginger until fragrant, about 1 minute. Add bok choy and soy sauce, stir-frying until bok choy is wilted but still crunchy, about 3-4 minutes.
4. Season bok choy stir-fry with salt and pepper. Serve alongside miso-glazed halibut.

Nutritional Facts (Per Serving): Calories: 380 | Fat: 12g | Carbohydrates: 15g | Protein: 50g | Fiber: 3g | Sugars: 7g | Sodium: 350mg

Blackened Swordfish with Mango Avocado Salsa

Prep: 20 minutes | Cook: 10 minutes | Serves: 4

Ingredients:

- 4 swordfish steaks (6 oz or 170g each)
- 2 tbsp olive oil (30ml)
- 1 tbsp blackening spice (15g)
- 1 mango, diced (200g)
- 1 avocado, diced (200g)
- 1/4 cup red onion, finely chopped (40g)
- 1 tbsp lime juice (15ml)
- Salt and pepper to taste
- Fresh cilantro for garnish (2 tbsp or 8g)

Instructions:

1. Rub swordfish steaks with olive oil and blackening spice. Season with salt and pepper.
2. Heat a skillet over medium-high heat and cook the steaks for 4-5 minutes per side.
3. Mix mango, avocado, red onion, lime juice, and cilantro for the salsa. Season with salt.
4. Serve swordfish topped with mango avocado salsa.

Nutritional Facts (Per Serving): Calories: 380 | Fat: 22g | Carbohydrates: 15g | Protein: 35g | Fiber: 5g | Sugars: 8g | Sodium: 200mg

Broiled Haddock with Spinach and Feta Salad

Prep: 15 minutes | Cook: 10 minutes | Serves: 4

Ingredients:

- 4 haddock fillets (6 oz or 170g each)
- 2 tbsp olive oil (30ml)
- 4 cups spinach (120g)
- 2 tbsp lemon juice (30ml)
- 1/2 cup feta cheese, crumbled (75g)
- Salt and pepper to taste
- Fresh dill for garnish (2 tbsp or 8g)

Instructions:

1. Preheat the broiler. Brush haddock with olive oil, season with salt and pepper. Broil for 8-10 minutes.
2. Toss spinach with lemon juice, feta cheese, salt, and pepper.
3. Serve haddock on a bed of spinach and feta salad, garnished with dill.

Nutritional Facts (Per Serving): Calories: 380 | Fat: 18g | Carbohydrates: 5g | Protein: 50g | Fiber: 2g | Sugars: 2g | Sodium: 400mg

Honey Mustard Glazed Trout with Green Beans

Prep: 15 minutes | Cook: 15 minutes | Serves: 4

Ingredients:

- 4 trout fillets (6 oz or 170g each)
- 2 tbsp honey (30ml)
- 2 tbsp Dijon mustard (30ml)
- 2 tbsp olive oil (30ml)
- 2 cups green beans, trimmed (200g)
- Salt and pepper to taste
- Lemon wedges for serving

Instructions:

1. Preheat oven to 375°F (190°C). Mix honey and mustard. Brush over trout.
2. Place trout on a lined baking sheet. Toss green beans with olive oil, salt, and pepper. Arrange around trout.
3. Bake for 12-15 minutes, until trout is cooked and green beans are tender.
4. Serve with lemon wedges.

Nutritional Facts (Per Serving): Calories: 380 | Fat: 16g | Carbohydrates: 15g | Protein: 45g | Fiber: 3g | Sugars: 10g | Sodium: 300mg

Paprika Spiced Sole with Roasted Garlic Broccoli

Prep: 20 minutes | Cook: 25 minutes | Serves: 4

Ingredients:

- 4 sole fillets (6 oz or 170g each)
- 2 tbsp olive oil (30ml)
- 1 tbsp paprika (6g)
- 4 cups broccoli florets (360g)
- 3 garlic cloves, minced (9g)
- Salt and pepper to taste
- Lemon wedges for serving

Instructions:

1. Preheat oven to 400°F (200°C). Toss broccoli with half the olive oil, garlic, salt, and pepper. Roast for 20 minutes.
2. Season sole with paprika, salt, and pepper. Heat remaining olive oil in a skillet over medium heat. Cook sole for 2-3 minutes per side.
3. Serve sole with roasted garlic broccoli and lemon wedges.

Nutritional Facts (Per Serving): Calories: 380 | Fat: 12g | Carbohydrates: 15g | Protein: 55g | Fiber: 4g | Sugars: 3g | Sodium: 200mg

CHAPTER 16: DINNER
Low-Carb Pastas and Risottos

Spaghetti Squash with Homemade Marinara Sauce

Prep: 10 minutes | Cook: 45 minutes | Serves: 4

Ingredients:

- 1 large spaghetti squash (800g), halved and seeds removed
- 1 tbsp olive oil (15ml)
- 3 cups tomato sauce (720ml)
- 1 garlic clove, minced (3g)
- 1 tbsp honey (15ml)
- 1 tsp dried basil (1g)
- Salt and pepper to taste
- Fresh basil for garnish

Instructions:

1. Preheat oven to 400°F (200°C). Brush the inside of the spaghetti squash with olive oil, season with salt and pepper, and roast cut-side down for 40 minutes.
2. Simmer tomato sauce, garlic, honey, basil, salt, and pepper over medium heat for 20 minutes.
3. Scrape the squash into strands with a fork and top with marinara sauce and fresh basil.

Nutritional Facts (Per Serving): Calories: 380 | Fat: 9g | Carbohydrates: 30g | Protein: 5g | Fiber: 6g | Sugars: 9g | Sodium: 500mg

Pasta alla Norma with Eggplant and Ricotta

Prep: 20 minutes | Cook: 30 minutes | Serves: 4

Ingredients:

- 8 oz whole wheat pasta (225g)
- 1 large eggplant, cubed (500g)
- 2 tbsp olive oil (30ml)
- 3 cups tomato sauce (720ml)
- 2 garlic cloves, minced (6g)
- 1/2 cup ricotta cheese (120g)
- Salt and pepper to taste
- Fresh basil for garnish

Instructions:

1. Cook pasta as directed, drain, and set aside.
2. Heat olive oil, cook eggplant for 10 minutes, then add garlic and cook 1 minute.
3. Stir in tomato sauce, simmer 15 minutes, and season.
4. Toss pasta with sauce, top with ricotta, and garnish with basil.

Nutritional Facts (Per Serving): Calories: 380 | Fat: 14g | Carbohydrates: 55g | Protein: 14g | Fiber: 11g | Sugars: 8g | Sodium: 600mg

Lemon and Asparagus Risotto

Prep: 10 minutes | Cook: 30 minutes | Serves: 4

Ingredients:

- 1 cup Arborio rice (200g)
- 4 cups vegetable broth (960ml)
- 1 tbsp olive oil (15ml)
- 1 small onion, finely chopped (100g)
- 1/2 cup grated Parmesan cheese (60g)
- 1 lb asparagus, trimmed and cut into 1-inch pieces (450g)
- 1 lemon, zested and juiced (30ml juice, 5g zest)
- Salt and pepper to taste

Instructions:

1. Heat olive oil in a large pan over medium heat. Add onion and cook until translucent, about 5 minutes.
2. Add Arborio rice and stir for 2 minutes. Gradually add vegetable broth, 1 cup at a time, stirring frequently until liquid is absorbed before adding more.
3. When rice is almost cooked, add asparagus, lemon zest, and lemon juice. Continue cooking until asparagus is tender.
4. Stir in Parmesan cheese. Season with salt and pepper.
5. Serve immediately, garnished with additional lemon zest if desired.

Nutritional Facts (Per Serving): Calories: 380 | Fat: 9g | Carbohydrates: 62g | Protein: 15g | Fiber: 4g | Sugars: 5g | Sodium: 700mg

Creamy Spinach and Mushroom Risotto (Cauliflower Rice)

Prep: 15 minutes | Cook: 20 minutes | Serves: 4

Ingredients:

- 4 cups cauliflower rice (400g)
- 2 tbsp olive oil (30ml)
- 1 small onion, finely chopped (100g)
- 2 cups spinach, chopped (60g)
- 1 cup mushrooms, sliced (70g)
- 2 garlic cloves, minced
- 1/2 cup Greek yogurt (120ml)
- Salt and pepper to taste
- 1/4 cup grated Parmesan cheese (30g)

Instructions:

1. Heat olive oil in a large skillet over medium heat.
2. Add onion and garlic, sauté until the onion is translucent, about 5 minutes.
3. Add mushrooms and cook until they begin to release their moisture and brown slightly, about 8 minutes.
4. Stir in cauliflower rice, cooking for another 5-7 minutes until it starts to soften. Mix in chopped spinach and cook until wilted, about 2-3 minutes.
5. Off heat, blend in Greek yogurt and Parmesan until creamy. Season with salt and pepper. Serve warm with extra Parmesan or herbs.

Nutritional Facts (Per Serving): Calories: 380 | Fat: 18g | Carbohydrates: 25g | Protein: 20g | Fiber: 5g | Sugars: 8g | Sodium: 300mg

CHAPTER 17: BONUSES

Meal Plans and Shopping Templates: Convenient Tools for Stress-Free Meal Planning.

To support your journey in managing Type 2 diabetes, we've created a 30-day grocery shopping guide tailored to the recipes in this cookbook. This guide simplifies meal preparation by focusing on wholesome, natural ingredients that help keep blood sugar levels stable, while minimizing processed foods. Be mindful of hidden sugars, especially in dressings and sauces. Adjust portion sizes to suit your individual needs, and enjoy the ease of planning healthy, diabetic-friendly meals. All ingredients listed are calculated for one person.

Grocery Shopping List for 7-Day Meal Plan

Meat

Turkey Bacon – 10 slices (for Turkey Bacon and Spinach Salad, Scramble)
Chicken Breast – 1 small (~170g / 6 oz) (for Grilled Chicken Salad, Lemon and Olive Chicken Stew)
Ground Chicken – 170g / 6 oz (for Cauliflower Shepherd's Pie)
Lamb Chops – 1 small (~170g / 6 oz) (for Lemon Herb Grilled Lamb Chops)

Fish

Cod Fillets – 1 fillet (~170g / 6 oz) (for Mediterranean-Style Baked Cod)
Haddock Fillet – 1 fillet (~170g / 6 oz) (for Herb-Crusted Haddock)
Flounder Fillets – 2 fillets (~170g / 6 oz each) (for Baked Stuffed Flounder)
Salmon Fillet – 1 fillet (~170g / 6 oz) (for Salmon en Papillote)

Vegetables

Spinach – 360g / 12 oz (for Egg Muffins, Salad, Scramble, Soup, Dip, Flounder, Shepherd's Pie)
Cherry Tomatoes – 300g / 10 oz (for Egg Muffins, Mediterranean Baked Cod)
Kale – 120g / 4 oz (for Egg Muffins)
Zucchini (Courgette) – 2 medium (~340g / 12 oz) (for Grilled Zucchini, Ratatouille)
Bell Peppers – 4 large (for Grilled Zucchini, Ratatouille, Salad)
Asparagus – 170g / 6 oz (for Lemon Herb Grilled Lamb Chops)
Cauliflower – 1 small (~500g / 18 oz) (for Shepherd's Pie)
Herbs (Fresh Basil, Parsley, Thyme, Dill) – Small bunch (~30g each) (for various dishes: Hummus, Ratatouille, Soup, etc.)
Garlic – 6 cloves (for various dishes: Ricotta, Cod, Shepherd's Pie)
Avocados – 3 medium (for Avocado Dip, Salad, Toast, Smoothie)
Lemons – 3 large (for various dishes: Ricotta Crepes, Chicken Stew, Hummus)

Fruits

Blueberries – 100g / 3.5 oz (for Ricotta Crepes, Frozen Yogurt)
Mixed Berries – 200g / 7 oz (for Smoothie, Pudding)
Lemon Zest – Zest from 1 lemon (for Ricotta Crepes)
Apples – 1 large (for Salad, Smoothie)
Dairy & Alternatives
Ricotta Cheese – 200g / 7 oz (for Ricotta Crepes, Pancakes)
Cottage Cheese – 120g / 4 oz (for Avocado and Cottage Cheese Dip)
Cream Cheese – 60g / 2 oz (for Cheesecake)
Feta Cheese – 120g / 4 oz (for Grilled Zucchini, Avocado Toast, Flounder)
Parmesan Cheese – 40g / 1.4 oz (for Hummus)
Blue Cheese – 30g / 1 oz (for Buffalo Chicken Salad)
Cheddar Cheese – 60g / 2 oz (for Baked Ricotta)
Almond Milk – 250ml / 8.5 fl oz (for Smoothie, Crepes, Pancakes)
Greek Yogurt – 200g / 7 oz (for Coconut and Chia Pudding)
Butter – 30g / 1 oz (for Pancakes, Ricotta)

Grains & Bread

Whole Wheat Tortilla – 1 small

(for Burrito)
Whole Grain Crackers – 1 small pack (~50g) (for Hummus)
Almond Flour – 60g / 2 oz (for Cheesecake, Pancakes)
Flaxseeds – 20g / 0.7 oz (for Smoothie)
Chia Seeds – 40g / 1.4 oz (for Energy Balls, Pudding)

Spices & Condiments

Olive Oil – 3 tablespoons (for various dishes: Baked Cod, Salad, Hummus)
Honey – 1 tablespoon (for Smoothie, Pancakes)
Balsamic Vinegar – 1 tablespoon (for Salad, Grilled Zucchini)
Cumin – 1 teaspoon (for Hummus)
Paprika – 1 teaspoon (for Shepherd's Pie)

Grocery Shopping List for 8-14 Day Meal Plan

Meat

Ground Turkey – 200g / 7 oz (for Turkey and White Bean Chili)
Beef – 170g / 6 oz (for Beef and Green Bean Stew)
Ground Chicken – 170g / 6 oz (for Meatloaf with Spinach)
Chicken Thighs – 1 (~170g / 6 oz) (for Baked Chicken Thighs with Salsa Verde)
Chicken Breast – 1 small (~170g / 6 oz) (for Caesar Salad)

Fish

Swordfish Fillet – 1 (~170g / 6 oz) (for Blackened Swordfish, Grilled Swordfish)
Sole Fillet – 1 (~170g / 6 oz) (for Paprika Spiced Sole)
Salmon Fillet – 1 (~170g / 6 oz) (for Smoked Salmon Omelette)
Sea Bass Fillet – 1 (~170g / 6 oz) (for Chilean Sea Bass with Pomegranate Salsa)

Vegetables

Spinach – 300g / 10 oz (for Ricotta Bake, Caesar Salad, Meatloaf, Frittata)
Portobello Mushrooms – 2 large (~170g / 6 oz each) (for Salad, Stuffed Peppers, Frittata)
Bell Peppers – 5 large (for Stuffed Peppers, Grilled Salad, Eggplant Salad, Salsa Verde)
Eggplant (Aubergine) – 1 medium (~170g / 6 oz) (for Grilled Eggplant Salad, Stew)
Arugula (Rocket) – 100g / 3.5 oz (for Portobello Mushroom Salad)
Swiss Chard – 150g / 5 oz (for Frittata)
Broccoli – 200g / 7 oz (for Broccoli and Couscous Salad, Roasted Broccoli)
Spaghetti Squash – 1 medium (~500g / 18 oz) (for Marinara Sauce)
Tomatoes – 4 large (for Stuffed Tomatoes, Marinara Sauce)
Mushrooms – 150g / 5 oz (for Bell Peppers, Frittata)
Green Beans – 100g / 3.5 oz (for Beef and Green Bean Stew)
Onions – 2 medium (for Stew, Meatloaf, Chili)
Garlic – 6 cloves (for Salsa Verde, Chili, Stuffed Peppers, Tapenade)
Lemons – 4 large (for Salsa, Tapenade, Mousse)
Thyme (Fresh) – Small bunch (~30g) (for Stuffed Peppers)
Cilantro (Fresh Coriander) – Small bunch (~30g) (for Salsa Verde, Mousse)

Fruits

Mixed Berries – 200g / 7 oz (for Parfait, Sherbet)
Avocados – 3 medium (for Avocado Mousse, Caesar Salad, Salsa)
Apples – 2 large (for Apple Cinnamon Quinoa Bowl, Salad)
Raspberries – 150g / 5 oz (for Raspberry Almond Scones)
Pomegranate Seeds – 50g / 1.7 oz (for Pomegranate Salsa)

Dairy & Alternatives

Ricotta Cheese – 200g / 7 oz (for Ricotta Bake, Pancakes)
Cottage Cheese – 100g / 3.5 oz (for Pancakes)
Feta Cheese – 150g / 5 oz (for Salad, Stuffed Tomatoes)
Cream Cheese – 60g / 2 oz (for Omelette, Stuffed Tomatoes)
Greek Yogurt – 200g / 7 oz (for Parfait)
Coconut Milk – 200ml / 7 fl oz (for Sherbet)
Almond Milk – 150ml / 5 fl oz (for Pancakes)
Butter – 30g / 1 oz (for Pancakes, Scones)
Cheddar Cheese – 50g / 1.7 oz (for Baked Chicken Thighs)

Grains & Bread

Quinoa – 80g / 3 oz (for Apple Cinnamon Quinoa Bowl)
Couscous – 60g / 2 oz (for Broccoli Couscous Salad, Pomegranate Salsa)
Almond Flour – 60g / 2 oz (for Scones, Peanut Butter Balls)

Spices & Condiments

Olive Oil – 4 tablespoons (for various dishes: Tapenade, Salads, Salsa Verde)
Honey – 1 tablespoon (for Pancakes)
Balsamic Vinegar – 1 tablespoon (for Salad, Grilled Eggplant Salad)
Paprika – 1 teaspoon (for Paprika Spiced Sole)

Cumin – 1 teaspoon (for Salsa Verde)
Mustard – 1 teaspoon (for Broccoli and Couscous Salad)
Chia Seeds – 40g / 1.4 oz (for Parfait)
Peanut Butter – 50g / 1.7 oz (for Peanut Butter Balls)

Grocery Shopping List for 15-21 Day Meal Plan

Meat

Pork Loin – 200g / 7 oz (for Pork Loin with Apples and Parsnips)
Ground Turkey – 170g / 6 oz (for Turkey Meatballs in Marinara Sauce)
Chicken Breast – 1 small (~170g / 6 oz) (for Caprese Salad with Grilled Chicken)
Turkey Bacon – 3 slices (for Cobb Salad)
Chicken Thighs – 1 small (~170g / 6 oz) (for Chicken Tikka Masala)
Beef – 170g / 6 oz (for Beef and Mushroom Stew)

Fish

Haddock Fillets – 1 fillet (~170g / 6 oz) (for Broiled Haddock)
Salmon Fillet – 1 fillet (~170g / 6 oz) (for Salmon Nicoise Salad)
Halibut Fillet – 1 fillet (~170g / 6 oz) (for Miso Glazed Halibut)
Tilapia Fillet – 1 fillet (~170g / 6 oz) (for Tilapia with Fennel and Orange Salad)

Vegetables

Spinach – 300g / 10 oz (for Broiled Haddock Salad, Frittata, Egg Muffins, Dip, Nicoise Salad)
Celery – 2 stalks (~100g / 3.5 oz) (for Smoothie, Stew)
Green Apples – 2 large (for Smoothie, Stew, Salad)
Cabbage – 100g / 3.5 oz (for Pork Stew)
Feta Cheese – 150g / 5 oz (for Spinach Salad, Frittata, Egg Muffins, Kale Salad)
Bell Peppers – 3 large (for Frittata, Salad, Curry)
Portobello Mushrooms – 2 large (~170g / 6 oz each) (for Grilled Mushrooms, Stew)
Bok Choy – 150g / 5 oz (for Miso Glazed Halibut)
Kale – 120g / 4 oz (for Kale Salad)
Zucchini (Courgette) – 1 large (~170g / 6 oz) (for Zucchini Noodles)
Tomatoes – 4 large (for Bisque, Nicoise Salad, Marinara Sauce)
Cauliflower – 1 small (~500g / 18 oz) (for Hash Browns)
Fennel Bulb – 1 small (~170g / 6 oz) (for Fennel and Orange Salad)
Basil (Fresh) – 1 small bunch (~30g) (for Bisque, Marinara Sauce)
Garlic – 6 cloves (for various dishes: Ricotta, Pork Stew, Curry)
Red Onion – 1 medium (~100g / 3.5 oz) (for Curry, Salad)

Fruits

Raspberries – 150g / 5 oz (for Friands)
Cranberries – 50g / 1.7 oz (for Cranberry Loaf)
Mixed Berries – 150g / 5 oz (for Smoothie)
Oranges – 2 large (for Loaf, Fennel Salad)

Dairy & Alternatives

Almond Milk – 200ml / 7 fl oz (for Oatmeal, Bisque)
Cottage Cheese – 100g / 3.5 oz (for Dip)
Ricotta Cheese – 150g / 5 oz (for Baked Ricotta)
Greek Yogurt – 100g / 3.5 oz (for Smoothie)
Cheddar Cheese – 50g / 1.7 oz (for Baked Ricotta)
Parmesan Cheese – 50g / 1.7 oz (for Zucchini Noodles)
Cream Cheese – 60g / 2 oz (for Egg Muffins, Dip)
Butter – 30g / 1 oz (for Lemon Bars, Loaf)

Grains & Bread

Rolled Oats – 80g / 3 oz (for Savory Oatmeal)
Basmati Rice – 60g / 2 oz (for Chicken Tikka Masala)
Brown Rice – 60g / 2 oz (for Lentil Curry)
Almond Flour – 60g / 2 oz (for Lemon Bars, Cookies, Cranberry Loaf)
Whole Wheat Tortilla – 1 small (for Quesadilla)
Breadcrumbs (Low-Carb) – 50g / 1.7 oz (for Meatballs)
Whole Wheat Crackers – 50g / 1.7 oz (for Ricotta)

Spices & Condiments

Chia Seeds – 40g / 1.4 oz (for Smoothie)
Olive Oil – 4 tablespoons (for various dishes: Roasted Pork, Curry, Salad)
Honey – 1 tablespoon (for Loaf, Smoothie)
Balsamic Vinegar – 1 tablespoon (for Caprese Salad, Salad Dressing)
Cumin – 1 teaspoon (for Curry, Salsa Verde)
Paprika – 1 teaspoon (for Tilapia, Hash Browns)
Miso Paste – 1 tablespoon (for Miso Oatmeal, Halibut)
Mustard – 1 teaspoon (for Salad Dressing)
Herbs (Thyme, Rosemary) – 1 small bunch (~30g) (for Pork Loin, Stew)

Grocery Shopping List for 22-28 Day Meal Plan

Meat

Ground Turkey – 170g / 6 oz (for Turkey Meatballs)
Chicken Breast – 2 small (~170g / 6 oz each) (for Grilled Chicken Salad, Spicy Chicken and Tomato Stew)
Beef Steak – 170g / 6 oz (for Steak Fajita Bowls)
Ground Chicken – 170g / 6 oz (for Zucchini Noodles with Turkey Meatballs)

Fish

Flounder Fillets – 2 (~170g / 6 oz each) (for Baked Stuffed Flounder with Spinach and Feta)
Salmon Fillet – 1 (~170g / 6 oz) (for Grilled Salmon with Avocado Salsa)
Haddock Fillet – 1 (~170g / 6 oz) (for Herb-Crusted Haddock)
Chilean Sea Bass – 1 (~170g / 6 oz) (for Chilean Sea Bass with Pomegranate Salsa)

Vegetables

Spinach – 300g / 10 oz (for Breakfast Burrito, Soup, Dip, Flounder)
Tomatoes – 5 large (for Caprese Salad, Stuffed Tomatoes, Salsa)
Eggplant (Aubergine) – 1 medium (~170g / 6 oz) (for Grilled Eggplant Salad, Ratatouille)
Bell Peppers – 3 large (for Grilled Eggplant Salad, Ratatouille)
Zucchini (Courgette) – 2 medium (~340g / 12 oz) (for Zucchini Noodles, Waffles)
Onions – 2 medium (for Soup, Stew, Salsa)
Garlic – 6 cloves (for various dishes: Dip, Tapenade, Stuffed Tomatoes)
Lemons – 3 large (for Tapenade, Salsa, Flatbread)
Celery – 2 stalks (~100g / 3.5 oz) (for Soup)
Avocado – 3 medium (for Salad, Salsa, Smoothie)
Blueberries – 100g / 3.5 oz (for Frozen Yogurt)
Broccoli – 200g / 7 oz (for Quiche, Steamed Vegetables)
Artichoke Hearts – 200g / 7 oz (for Dip)
Fresh Thyme – 1 small bunch (~30g) (for Tapenade, Salsa)

Fruits

Mixed Berries – 150g / 5 oz (for Smoothie)
Raspberries – 100g / 3.5 oz (for Friands)
Pomegranate Seeds – 50g / 1.7 oz (for Salsa)

Dairy & Alternatives

Egg Whites – 6 large (for Breakfast Burrito, Waffles)
Feta Cheese – 150g / 5 oz (for Burrito, Caprese Salad, Flounder, Stuffed Tomatoes)
Cheddar Cheese – 120g / 4 oz (for Quiche, Waffles)
Cream Cheese – 60g / 2 oz (for Stuffed Tomatoes)
Greek Yogurt – 100g / 3.5 oz (for Coconut and Chia Seed Pudding)
Almond Milk – 200ml / 7 fl oz (for Smoothies, Pudding)
Goat Cheese – 60g / 2 oz (for Flatbread)

Grains & Bread

Whole Wheat Tortilla – 1 small (for Breakfast Burrito)
Brown Rice – 60g / 2 oz (for Fajita Bowls, Salsa)
Whole Grain Couscous – 60g / 2 oz (for Pomegranate Salsa and Couscous)
Almond Flour – 60g / 2 oz (for Cake, Friands)
Chia Seeds – 40g / 1.4 oz (for Pudding, Frozen Yogurt)
Flaxseeds – 30g / 1 oz (for Smoothie)

Spices & Condiments

Olive Oil – 3 tablespoons (for various dishes: Salsa, Flatbread, Fajita Bowls)
Balsamic Vinegar – 1 tablespoon (for Caprese Salad)
Cumin – 1 teaspoon (for Salsa, Tapenade)
Honey – 1 tablespoon (for Cake)
Almond Extract – 1 teaspoon (for Cake)
Paprika – 1 teaspoon (for Stew, Tapenade)

Printed in Great Britain
by Amazon